GOD WITH US

VAN BOGARD DUNN

GRADED PRESS
NASHVILLE, TENNESSEE

GOD WITH US

A study book

Copyright © 1967 by Graded Press

☐ Henry M. Bullock is editor of church school publica-
tions, Editorial Division, Methodist Board of Education.
☐ Horace R. Weaver is editor of adult publications.
☐ Harold L. Fair is editor of Foundation Studies in
Christian Faith, the series of which this book is the
second volume.

TO GERRY

CONTENTS

EDITOR'S INTRODUCTION

The book you are now reading is the second study book in a new curriculum series, Foundation Studies in Christian Faith. A new part (or unit) will be issued three months from the publication of this part and for each succeeding three months until eight parts have been published. The other seven parts are described on the inside front cover of this book. The series—Foundation Studies in Christian Faith —therefore is an eight-part study that may extend for two years if a new part is begun every three months.

The components. There are three "components" to each part of the study:

—the study book (which you are now reading)
—the book of selected readings
—the resource packet for leaders of adult groups

These three components make up one part. Each three months a new study book, a new book of selected readings, and a new resource packet for leaders of adult groups will be issued. The three components in each quarterly part have the same title. For example, the book of selected readings and the resource packet to accompany this book are also entitled *God With Us.*

The study book. As you turn through this study book, you will notice several distinguishing features. At the beginning of each chapter, reference is made to a biblical passage which will be the basis for study of that chapter. Read this passage in your Bible before you read the chapter. We recommend the *Oxford Annotated Bible,* Revised Standard Version (Oxford University Press) or the *Harper Study Bible,* Revised Standard Version (published by Zondervan Publishing House) for home use by every member of the class. (Available from Cokesbury.) When you come to an asterisk (*), turn to the end of the chapter. There you will find the notes, which give the source of the quotations.

Leadership procedures. You will notice as you look through this book that certain paragraphs have a small black square (■) at the beginning. These paragraphs suggest a wide variety of ways of reacting to the ideas raised in the material. It is not expected that a group will use every suggestion or procedure. The procedures are placed in the study book to encourage each member of the group to assume responsibility for discussion and to stimulate thinking as you read the book. There is no separate book for leaders only. Leaders and other members of the group should each have personal copies of both the study book and the book of selected readings. Only the designated leader or "teaching team," however, will receive the resource packet described below for use with the group. The packet contains a leaders' guide.

The book of selected readings. Each person in the group should have a copy of the book of selected readings with the same title as this study book, *God With Us.* In the book of selected readings, you will find a wide variety of selections from a number of other printed resources relevant to the study of the Bible as witness to the good news. While it is not absolutely essential for every person to have a copy of the

8

book of selected readings, the study will be significantly enriched if this study book and the book of selected readings are read and used together. They are companion volumes. Many procedures involve use of selected readings. In this study book you will frequently see the abbreviation *S/R* followed by a number. When you come to a place in the text where this abbreviation appears, turn to the book of selected readings and find the reading whose number corresponds to the one following the abbreviation *S/R*. The book of selected readings has no page numbers—rather, the selections are numbered. Reading and discussion of these selections will greatly stimulate study of this unit.

The resource packet. In addition to a new study book and a new book of selected readings each three months, a resource packet for leaders will be issued, having the same title as the study book and the book of selected readings. Each group will need one packet with the same title as this study book, *God With Us.* Each packet contains a variety of resources for use by the leader with the group: filmslips, records, pictures, maps, charts, and the like. The packet will also contain a leaders' guide to suggest how the materials in the packet may best be used with the group. Each person in the group should have a study book and a book of selected readings; but only one packet will be needed for the group.

Covenant groups. Individuals in each group may wish to make a covenant with one another regarding this study. In this covenant, each person would agree to read the books faithfully in preparation for each discussion session and to be faithful in attendance and participation in the group meetings. Some covenant groups may wish to work out an agreement each person would be asked to sign; other groups may make the pledge without a formal agreement.

Leaders. The success of this two-year study depends in large measure on the leadership of the group. Some groups may wish to have a different leader or team with each new

9

part of the study. Other groups may wish to divide each part, so that one person or couple takes responsibility for one or more sessions. Each person in the group should realize that faithful preparation and participation are essential if the goal of the study is to be achieved. The designated leaders alone cannot and should not take the sole responsibility for the outcome of the study; this responsibility must be shared by all members of the group.

Imagination. Groups who approach this study with imagination will find that the study may go on longer than the thirteen weeks of a quarter of the year. Do not feel that this study must be completed in three months. Your group might wish to extend the study to a longer period. Some chapters may be combined for one discussion session, others expanded to more than one. The series may be used in many settings other than on Sunday mornings. Use of the imagination will add liveliness and interest to the search for faith. The use of music, art, and other resources will make the search for faith more meaningful.

The editorial team that developed this unit was Lon A. Speer (resource packet), Judith Weidman (book of selected readings), Harold D. Minor and Nellie Moser (leadership procedures), Mary Alice Asbury (manuscript editor), and Horace R. Weaver. Dan Brawner and Richard Elliott were responsible for the design and layout. Mrs. Jeanne Arnold faithfully typed and retyped the manuscript.

HAROLD L. FAIR

AUTHOR'S PREFACE

I have written this book under the pressures of my daily life at home and on the job. I might have written it differently if I had been able to retreat into some research center where I would have been protected from the claims of my routine obligations; but now that it is finished, I am glad that it was written in just this way. I am glad because I have had to write the way most of my readers will have to read this book—under the pressures of family and work. So I invite my readers to join me in a kind of Bible study which is not a retreat from our rich and crowded ways of life but which is a call to a fuller and more meaningful participation in that life.

The biblical passages I have considered in this book have spoken decisively to me of the power and presence of God in our lives. In developing each chapter, I have tried to let the witness of the biblical narrative speak to the reader through the words of the text. I have offered my own interpretation as clearly and honestly as possible, not because I claim to have *the* correct interpretation but because I feel

11

that all of us must make a faithful decision about what we hear proclaimed in the biblical witness. My purpose throughout the book has been to share with my readers in a personal and immediate study of the biblical witness, so that together we will experience what God is saying and doing in our time.

At every stage in my interpretation, I have attempted to understand the good news of God's presence in relation to our daily lives. I have done this because I am convinced that responsible Bible study demands that we see God's presence with us not only in our "religious" experiences but in the whole range of our humanity. As we study the biblical witness, we are helped to see that God gives himself to us to free us from all that prevents our being truly human. My hope for this book is that it will help us to participate in a community of Bible study in which we will experience the fullness of God's grace at the point of all our needs.

In all that I have tried to affirm in these pages I acknowledge that I have been "surrounded by . . . a cloud of witnesses." For all that I have consciously and unconsciously borrowed from them I am deeply grateful. There are two in this host of witnesses whose memory has been ever before me, my father and mother, Knox G. and Mary Bogard Dunn. From them I first heard the good news; through them I first saw that God is with us.

VAN BOGARD DUNN

Methodist Theological School in Ohio
Delaware, Ohio

A CHECKLIST

Study a Portion of the Bible

(If your answer is "yes," check the appropriate square.)

	Chapter 1: Genesis 2:4b–3:24	Chapter 2: Exodus 32	Chapter 3: Amos 3	Chapter 4: Matthew 1:18-25	Chapter 5: Luke 4:16-30	Chapter 6: Acts 10:1–11:18	Chapter 7: Mark 14:12-25	Chapter 8: Philippians 2:1-11	Chapter 9: Mark 14:26-72; 16:1-8	Chapter 10: Acts 26:1-23	Chapter 11: Ephesians 4:1-16	Chapter 12: Romans 8:28-39

I. Have you consulted these helps:
—a commentary?
—an atlas?
—a Bible dictionary?
—at least one modern translation?

II. Have you tried to discover about the writer (s) :
—his historical and personal circumstances at the time of writing?
—his intended audience?
—his purpose in writing?
—his choice of literary form?
—his central message and characteristic emphases?

III. Have you tried to learn about the first readers:
—who they were?
—their historical and personal circumstances?
—their language, culture, religious background, and social traits?
—their characteristic point of view about the writer's subject matter?

IV. Have you understood the key ideas and words of the passage:
—their central message?
—their relation to other key ideas within the book?
—their relation to other key ideas within the whole Bible?
—their relative and continuing value in the light of Jesus Christ?

V. Have you asked yourself:
—What would it mean for me to *live* and *act* in the light of this passage?

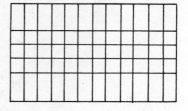
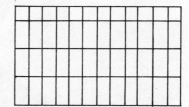
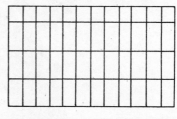
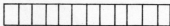

Adam by Rodin

Read in your Bible:
Genesis 2:4b–3:24

1

□□

WHAT HAS GONE WRONG?

The front page of our local newspaper is spread out on
my desk. As I glance down the columns the following headlines catch my attention: "Russian-Red China Split Now
Out in Open," "China Bars Soviet Aircraft," "Pravda Calls
for Rebuff," "Inez' Brawling Gales Slash Into Gulf Coast,"
"Russian, American Top-Level Talks Set," "Two Columbus
Men Held in Circleville," "Allied Troops Pressing Three-
Pronged Attack," and "Freeway Section Completed." The
lead in each story makes it clear that the front page on this
particular day was dominated by bad news. Four of the
stories report international tension; one, the war in Viet
Nam; one, a hurricane; one, a crime; and one, the construc-
tion of a highway. Only the last can qualify as good news.

■ *In the room where your group is meeting, display a large poster on which
are written assignments for specific preparation to be made by the members
of the group before the session begins.*

15

Today's paper was not unusual. Any other day would show about the same thing. Take a quick look at the headlines on the front page of your own newspaper. The chances are good that you will find most of the space devoted to bad news. Some of this may result from our human interest in bad news. Even after allowances have been made, however, an average day in our history is marked by national and international conflict, natural calamity, and crime. These things are not *unusual*.

War, disaster, and crime are clearly not *normal* in the sense that they agree with an accepted standard of what ought to be. They may be part of our daily experience, but they always come upon us as bad news. The very fact that we label the reports of wars, disasters, and crimes as "bad news" is evidence that we view such things as evils in human history. *The bad news on the front pages of our newspapers is not just a sign of the times. It is also a sign that something has gone wrong in our lives.* (S/R, 1.)

In this regard the Bible has much in common with the front pages of our newspapers. The narratives in the Bible often report bad news about the human situation. The history of Israel in the Old Testament and the life of Jesus and the beginnings of church history in the New Testament contain reports of war, distress, and crime that are as realistic and frank as anything we might see, hear, or read today. The Bible, like the front pages of our newspapers, reports that something has gone wrong with the human situation. The Bible and our common experiences are closely related. This is true even of our experiences of tragedy and failure. Of course, bad news is not the only point of contact between the ancient world of the Bible and our modern world of space exploration. But we can easily recognize that bad news provides a bridgehead for beginning this study together. (S/R, 2.)

■ One procedure for each chapter suggests that your group set goals. To help you get started the study committee or leadership team might pose a question that, on the basis of study and planning, expresses the main concern of the chapter. Now, as a group, ask yourselves: (1) What should we learn to help us find some answers to this question? and (2) What should we do after we have found some answers? By your answers to these two questions, you will have set your goals for learning both content and behavior. Go through these steps as you begin the study of each new chapter, using a guiding question appropriate to the chapter.

THE BAD NEWS IN THE BIBLE

Our newspapers report the bad news in specific stories about concrete events. It is not reported in general statements. This is also true of the biblical narratives. The Bible as a whole does not teach general truths about the human situation. It contains the written record of a specific people (Israel) whose history is composed of concrete events (such as the Exodus). We must never lose sight of the fact that the books we call the Bible are the result of a literary process which began about 1000 B.C. and ended about A.D. 150. First the Israelites and then the early Christians passed the accounts of events from one generation to the next by talking, writing, editing, collecting, and preserving the end product as sacred literature. (See, for example, II Chronicles 36, where a source book for the history of Israel and Judah is mentioned.) When we turn to the Bible to see what is wrong in the human situation, we do not find theories about the origin of evil. We meet with the written records of men struggling to resist the threat of war, distress, crime, and the persistent concerns in life.

One such record is found in Genesis 2:4b–3:24, the familiar story of the garden of Eden. This narrative tells how Adam and Eve disobeyed God and were banished from the garden forever.

■ Use Conversation Two from "Six Conversations" (Resource Packet, item 3). The Leaders' Guide in the packet suggests ways to use these brief bits of dialogue. Some questions to guide your consideration: (1) What makes a person sure that his view is the right one? (2) On what grounds do the opposing speakers base their opinions? (3) How can we judge the truth of the viewpoints expressed in these conversations?

■ As a total group, discuss one or both of these questions: (1) In what ways is the Bible like the daily paper, and in what ways unlike it? (2) Why are we interested in bad news—in the Bible or in the paper? (3) How is the story of Adam and Eve our story?

WHEN WAS IT WRITTEN?

One of the first steps in interpreting Genesis 2:4b–3:24 is to discover how it fits in with the centuries-long literary process that resulted in the Bible as we now know it. To find out where it fits, we must draw upon conclusions that have been reached by experts in Old Testament life and literature.

Scholars today are generally agreed that Genesis was not written by a single author. Instead, it was produced by an inspired collector who gathered together separate documents and edited them so that they became a unified work.

On the basis of historical and critical study of the Hebrew text of Genesis it is now possible to identify at least three different documents that have gone into the composition of the book. These three documents have been woven into a single story found in the books of Genesis, Exodus, Leviticus, Numbers, and Joshua. These documents are identified by the distinctive characteristics of their subject matter. The J document is so called because its customary name for God is *Jahweh* (pronounced as Yahweh), which is usually translated "Lord" in the Revised Standard Version of the Bible. The E document derives its name from the fact that it characteristically refers to God as *Elohim*. And P is so designated because its subject matter deals with the doctrinal concerns of the *priests* who served in the Jerusalem temple. Thus the letters J, E, and P are used as a kind of "shorthand" to refer to the three documents that have been combined

18

to produce the Book of Genesis. (*S/R,* 3.) These sources plus the D document (Deuteronomy) form the basic resources used in the first six books of the Old Testament.

■ Use "Three Sources of Exodus 7:14-24" (Resource Packet, item 4). The Leaders' Guide in the packet contains suggestions for its use. Also see *S/R,* 3 for an interpretive resource.

To which of these three documents does Genesis 2:4*b*–3:24 belong? One key is the use of the word *Lord* throughout the narrative. A glance at a concordance that gives the Hebrew for the word translated *Lord* will show that it is based on the word *Jahweh* ("Yahweh"), the name for God in the J document. Therefore, this narrative belongs to the J document. What is the significance of this conclusion? Simply this: the J document, including Genesis 2:4*b*–3:24, will tell us something about the concerns of the time, just as almost anything written in the United States in 1941-45 would reflect World War II. The date generally accepted for the J document is 930 B.C., and it is usually linked to the tribe of Judah. Genesis 2:4*b*–3:24 is a searching criticism of the reign of Solomon and is intended to urge Solomon to renew and re-establish the covenant relationship.

The year 930 B.C. is an unusually well-documented period in the history of Israel. It falls in the reign of King Solomon, but the figure who dominates the scene even after his death is the great King David.

The author of the J document had been profoundly influenced by David's military genius and political skill. He had reflected at length upon the significance of the events of the past: the uniting of the twelve tribes into one nation, the defeat of the Philistines and Canaanites, and the setting up of Jerusalem as the capital city of the united monarchy. What did these events mean? What he saw forced him to affirm that the center of God's activity in Israel was no longer the religious celebrations at the various shrines; to understand

19

the activity of God, one must include the whole life of the people. He must look at the nation's past, but there is something more.

The writer of the J document began to search the inner life of man to find evidences of God's activity. The affairs of the heart became more meaningful to him than the rites of the altar. What took place at the shrines was not ignored, but he focused his attention on the public and private lives of men. (*S/R,* 4.)

As we look closely at the story of the garden of Eden, we find that the author of the J document has given us a vivid description of the whole sweep of human experience. The setting of the action is not a religious shrine or a sacred place but the garden that God prepared for man in Eden (Genesis 2:4*b*-9).

The garden is not a particular place that can be found geographically. The attempts to locate it on the basis of information given in Genesis 2:10-14 have all proved useless. The garden is a symbol that the writer used to represent the inhabited earth. This is an important point to keep in mind as we attempt to relate this passage of Scripture to our own lives. Once we recognize that the author was not describing a particular place in the ancient world, we are free to see that the garden is the place where we live and make the choices that determine our destiny. Their story is our story.

MAN IS A CREATURE

What are the main features of this story? Do they really reflect our own experiences?

The story begins with a picture of the earth without life, awaiting the creation of man (Genesis 2:4*b*-6). At first, this appears to have no meaning for our modern world. But on second thought these verses affirm that the center of all creation is human life. There is no meaning without the conscious life of man. The conscious life of man does not arise from the other forms of created life. "The LORD God formed man of dust from the ground, and breathed into his nostrils the breath of life; and man became a living being" (Genesis 2:7). Man is set over against all other creatures. The more we study the more our knowledge supports the assertion that man is "a living being" different from every other form of life. (S/R, 5.)

■ Read silently S/R, 1 and 5. Then in small groups discuss these questions: From the study book, the selected readings, contemporary science, and your own experience, what evidence do you have that human life is the center of all creation? What evidence that it is not? What difference does it make to you?

Genesis 2 teaches that the life of man is to be understood as a part of creation. This means that, although human life is the center of creation, man shares in the limitations of all other creatures. He is not the Creator; he is not God; but rather he is a creature, dependent upon God. This is expressed throughout the narrative but most powerfully in Genesis 2:16-17: "You may freely eat of every tree of the garden; but of the tree of the knowledge of good and evil you shall not eat, for in the day that you eat of it you shall die."

The force of this commandment comes through at two points. (1) It affirms that the life which man enjoys is the result of God's gracious provision for his needs. (2) It asserts that man's enjoyment of what God has provided is conditioned by his recognition of his creaturely dependence upon God. The command not to eat "of the tree of the knowledge of good and evil" supports this last point. "The tree of knowledge of good and evil" does not, it seems to me, refer to the ability to make moral distinctions between good and evil. Many scholars believe that "the knowledge of good and evil" is a symbol of the attempt to know everything, to live independently of God.

The fundamental meaning of Genesis 2:16-17 is: Be truly human in obedient dependence upon God, and you shall live; but if you deny your true humanity in rebellion against God, you shall die.

This brings us to an important observation about the description of human life in Genesis 2:4b–3:24. What was the basic assumption of the writer? He believed that he and his people were living their lives before God. The background for what he wrote in Genesis 2:4b–3:24 is the whole sweep of Israel's relationship with the living God: the deliverance from Egypt, the covenant at Mount Sinai, the occupation of Canaan, and the establishment of the united monarchy. In this narrative he is proclaiming that the true life of man is realized in faithful dependence upon the God who has revealed his gracious care in the experiences of Israel.

This viewpoint is immediately relevant to our own attempt to describe our daily lives in the last third of the twentieth century. What we see is always conditioned by our point of view, by our understanding of our past. Perhaps the most important thing the author of Genesis 2:4b–3:24 has done for us is to raise a fundamental question for us. What is our point of view? If we assume that there is nothing in the life of man that stands over against man as his Creator and Judge and Redeemer, then these chapters from Genesis have no meaning for us. On the other hand, if we share the author's faith in the living God, then his story of Adam and Eve in the garden of Eden helps us to see that the most important factor in our life is our relationship to God. (S/R, 6.)

■ Let a person prepared in advance read aloud S/R, 7. An additional possibility would be to play the story of creation from the recording of *God's Trombones* by James Weldon Johnson (available at record shops). Then let each member, who will, respond to these expressions of faith—by a personal witness, a prayer, a verse of Scripture or poetry, a hymn, or other expression of personal relationship to God.

22

ANALYSIS OF THE HUMAN SITUATION

The author of the story of Adam and Eve saw that something had gone wrong to prevent man's enjoyment of what God had provided for him. In this narrative he was struggling not merely with the question of *what* had gone wrong but with the more difficult question of *why*.

Our earlier analogy of the newspaper may help us to clarify this distinction. The news stories in a newspaper report *what* has happened. The bad news on the front pages of our community newspapers is composed of such stories. But the editors of our newspapers are not content just to report *what*. They have a point of view that tends to color their reporting of news events, and this point of view is stated clearly on the editorial pages. There the editors analyze the news from their points of view and state *why* things are the way they are.

Likewise in this narrative the author attempted to tell *why* Adam and Eve had been banished from the garden of Eden. He took great care to make sure that he was not misunderstood. First, he made it plain that God was in no way responsible. He did this by affirming again and again the goodness of God revealed in his gracious care for man. God's relationship to man was life giving and life sustaining (Genesis 2:7-8, 18-24). The depth of God's concern for man was disclosed in the fact that he made woman to provide "a helper fit for him" (Genesis 2:18-24).

Second, the author insists that there was no fault in creation itself that could account for what had gone wrong in the human situation. The inhabited earth was formed and sustained by the good God. Therefore, it was good and not evil (Genesis 2:8). All man's relationships were good: his relationship to the life-giving land, his relationship to other living creatures, and the relationship between man and woman. Sexuality was not some fatal desire in the dark

23

caverns of human existence. It was the good gift of God to provide for the fulfillment of man's life. "Therefore a man leaves his father and his mother and cleaves to his wife, and they become one flesh" (Genesis 2:24).

Why then had things gone wrong in the garden of Eden? From start to finish, the author focused his attention squarely upon man. He was determined in all that he wrote to let nothing detract from his belief that man himself was responsible for his failure to enjoy what God had given him. In 3:1-7 the conversations between the woman and the serpent and the woman and her husband were used by the writer to show that man chose in his own heart to turn away from God in disobedience.

The author, who was writing in the days of King Solomon, believed that everything that had gone wrong was the result of this act of disobedience. Man's relationship to God had been transformed from confident trust to fear and shame. "The man and his wife hid themselves from the presence of the LORD God among the trees of the garden" (Genesis 3:8b). The breaking of this fundamental relationship had corrupted all other relationships.

Sin had broken the community of creation. Therefore, enmity prevailed between the woman and the serpent (Genesis 3:14-15). Pain and subjection became the lot of woman in her relationship to her husband (Genesis 3:16). And man was given the burden of unremitting toil (Genesis 3:17-19). (S/R, 8.)

This narrative is a carefully developed description and analysis of the life of man from the standpoint of faith in the living God. When we read it in comparison with the bad news reported on the front pages of our newspapers, we are led to ask: How does it help us to understand our daily lives? (1) It helps us to see that God's purpose in creation is that human life should be fulfilled and perfected. Any event in

24

human history that prevents the fulfillment and perfection must be seen as bad news. (2) The events occurring in our experience that prevent our enjoyment of God and his creation cannot be blamed on God or on any part of his creation. (3) The worst news is simply that we have chosen to disobey God, to deny our dependence on God and his creation, and to live in sin rather than in faith. (4) Every specific report of something wrong in the human situation is a consequence of our fundamental rebellion against God. Study of this Scripture suggests that we read the front pages of our newspapers as significant reports of our disobedient lives. (S/R, 9.)

■ Four ways are listed in the previous paragraph in which our Bible passage (Genesis 2:4b–3:24), read against the background of today's newspaper, helps us understand our lives. In small groups select from a newspaper specific reports of something wrong. Let each group tell how its example is, or is not, a "consequence of our fundamental rebellion against God," as in the fourth statement above.

Most of us have had experiences of human relationships that shed light on the description and analysis of the human situation in Genesis 2:4b–3:24. Perhaps the most common is romantic attachment for a person of the opposite sex. When one is in love, his whole life centers in and is dependent upon the object of his love. Every other relationship is dependent upon the condition of that fundamental relationship. If something happens to disturb or break that relationship, then the whole created order is transformed from a garden of happiness to a desert of sorrow.

By this comparison I mean to suggest that the proper way to pursue the study of this Scripture is to center our attention upon what it tells us about the fundamental relationships of *our* lives. This narrative is a penetrating portrayal and diagnosis of the way human life has been and is experienced *now* in relationship to God and his creation.

GOOD NEWS: GOD IN THE HUMAN SITUATION

Our study of Genesis 2:4b–3:24 is not completed by noting the consequences of our sin against God. We must now consider the closing verses in which the author proclaimed his faith that God had not left Adam and Eve to perish in the tragedy of their disobedience.

Man's sin did not triumph over God's goodness nor did it destroy completely the supporting grace of God's creation. Life continued in spite of man's rebellion against God. "The man called his wife's name Eve, because she was the mother of all living" (Genesis 3:20). Life was not perfect, but it had to be lived. The author saw that man's sin had not separated him completely from God's care.

The writer also wanted to express the fact that man's rebellion had so corrupted his capacity for faith that man himself was unable to return to Paradise. Thus he wrote: "At the east of the garden of Eden he placed the cherubim, and a flaming sword which turned every way, to guard the way to the tree of life" (Genesis 3:24). The writer understood that man could not return to the paradise he had lost. So he did not hold any hope for a return to the "good old days." The only life that remained for man was the life which opened up "east of the garden of Eden," the life marred by the broken relationships caused by man's disobedience.

Let us look now at the bad news that is so characteristic of our daily existence. In the light of the story of Adam and Eve we are able to see clearly that the broken relationships of our lives have not separated us completely from God's care and have not destroyed the fundamental goodness of God's creation. In the midst of life's imperfections life is precious. And although life may be hard, it is sustained by the gracious providence of God. Even east of Eden, surrounded by threats to human life, we till God's good earth and by the sweat of our faces eat our bread.

This does not mean that we ignore the tragic consequences

26

of our sin. Judgment is a fact of our daily lives. It screams across the front pages of our newspapers. But that judgment is evidence that God will not compromise with what we have done with our lives.

The good news is that God has not accepted the bad news as the last word about our human history.

We know from our human experiences that once we break a relationship of confidence and trust we cannot go back to the way things were. No matter how desperately I may desire to restore a broken relationship, I cannot alone make things right. I am at the mercy of the other person and have to go forward with him, hoping that through a new act of trust he will give himself to me so that we can be together again. This is a parable of our life with God east of Eden. We cannot work our way back into the garden of Eden. Sin has corrupted our capacity for faith ("the cherubim, and a flaming sword") ; man alone cannot restore his broken relationship with God. But we should not lose heart. We should go forward into the life that God has given us, hopeful that he will deepen this new relationship which will fulfill all his purposes for our lives.

■ A previously recruited group may have read S/R, 9. They have planned how to act out a situation that illustrates some broken relationship resulting from the dehumanization of man and some attempt to restore this relationship. Can you see any signs of God's activity in this attempt?

■ Close with one person reading as a benediction the last two paragraphs of S/R, 7.

■ Let the leadership team be prepared to make assignments for the next chapter of study and the members of the group be prepared to accept the assignments.

27

"They say they are wise, but they are fools." Romans 1:22

2

□□

A STIFF-NECKED PEOPLE

Whom or what do you trust? Life itself raises this question. We cannot exist without trusting persons and things. The relationships that sustain us in our families and our work are based upon mutual trust and confidence. The most routine transactions, such as depositing money in a bank or servicing an automobile, require that we commit our resources and our safety to the care of other persons. Whenever we cannot trust others and they cannot trust us, the processes of life are interrupted and sometimes brought to a standstill. We see signs of the breakdown of trust in broken homes, crime, racial tension, international disputes, and war.

So when we raise the question of faith or trust, we are considering an issue whose outcome determines the quality of

■ *As you arrive at your place of meeting, check the assignment chart for specific preparation to be made before the session begins.*

■ Set goals for your study of this chapter as suggested on page 17.

our lives. One of man's most pressing problems is how to be trusting and trustworthy. Who among us would claim that he is completely trustworthy? Most of us are haunted- by the memory of trust betrayed. This is our predicament: we must live by faith, yet we are never completely free from that basic distrust of ourselves and others. This distrust threatens to make us untrustworthy persons.

The problem of trust is one of the central themes of the Bible. But it is never discussed there merely as an idea or a theory. The Bible tells us about faith by telling the words and deeds of men and women who struggled with the fundamental issues of life. So as we turn to the Bible to find strength and guidance for our own lives we do not force our modern concerns upon the ancient texts. Instead, we find that the centuries fall away before our common humanity. Wherever men and women are engaged in the eternal problems, there we meet our own lives and history. (S/R, 10.)

I have chosen Exodus 32 as the basis for this chapter because it shows how the Bible deals with the problem of man's faith.

■ To gain a panoramic view of the persons and events in Israel's history, study "A Timeline of the Biblical Story" (Resource Packet, item 5). Your leadership team should consult the Leaders' Guide in the packet for suggestions for using the timeline.

■ In pairs discuss for five minutes: What evidence do you see that if we cannot trust we cannot be trusted? What is your understanding of "the danger of giving absolute trust to some person or thing"? How would you begin to determine who or what you can trust? Share any insights with the group.

■ Five persons (four characters and a narrator) may introduce the Scripture, Exodus 32, by reading it as a playlet. They may wish to rewrite it ahead of time as simple dialogue.

■ A resource person (Bible scholar, minister, or a member of the group assigned in advance) may illustrate the importance of understanding the context to proper interpretation of Scripture by pointing out the possibilities of misinterpretation of particular passages. (For example: Genesis 9:25-27; 2 Samuel 12:1-15; Isaiah 7:14.)

GOD MAKES AN AGREEMENT WITH HIS PEOPLE

One helpful rule of biblical study is that each verse usually must be understood in relationship to what is written before and after it. This also applies to most chapters. They are to be read against the background of the entire book in which they are found. This is certainly true of Exodus 32.

The chapter does not stand alone. It belongs to a unit of material that begins with Exodus 19 and continues through Numbers 10. These chapters were probably produced over a long period of time by a number of different writers. But they all have one thing in common: they witness to the meaning of the relationship that was established between God and Israel at Mount Sinai.

Many years after the Israelites sought relief from famine in Egypt, "there arose a new king over Egypt, who did not know Joseph" (Exodus 1:8). The Israelites were forced to serve the Egyptians as slaves and were threatened with extermination. God saw the affliction of his people and raised up Moses to deliver them from their bondage.

As we read the material in Exodus 19 through Numbers 10, the one word that gives it unity and purpose is *covenant*. (*S/R*, 11.) At Mount Sinai, God made a covenant with Israel that became the basis for a new relationship between the people and their God. Through the covenant, God became their God and they became his people (Exodus 6:7; Leviticus 26:12; Deuteronomy 26:17-19).

The word *covenant* is used in a variety of ways in the Old Testament. When it refers to the special relationship established between God and Israel at Mount Sinai, it usually means these four things. (1) The covenant was a solemn agreement between two unequal parties: God the superior and Israel the inferior. (2) The agreement was not something that Israel thought up and arranged with God. (3) It originated with God and was offered by him to the people as an expression of his loving care for them. (4) The role

31

of the people in the agreement was to receive it and to enjoy the communion with God that it offered.

The covenant or agreement at Mount Sinai was God's good gift to Israel which assured the total well-being of the people.

Here is a type of experience that many of us have shared that will help to clarify the meaning of the covenant God made with Israel. Many of us have depended upon some person whose authority was the most important factor in determining our well-being. Of course, we are never inactive in such a relationship, but the basic nature of the relationship is primarily dependent upon the attitude and actions of the one placed over us. (For instance, the nature of a relationship of the boss to an employee is determined by the boss.) Usually the superior initiates the agreement and offers it to us as the basis of our relationship to him.

Obviously, this comparison of the agreement between God and Israel with the agreement between a superior and those placed under him cannot be pushed too hard. For one thing, no human superior ever has the absolute control of another individual that God exercises over all creation. But the comparison is useful because it helps us to see the agreement in the light of a common human experience and because it emphasizes the fact that God *made* the agreement and Israel *received* it.

The way God revealed himself to Israel was by giving the people his law. Our English word *law* usually suggests a legal code. To the writer of the narratives about the agreement at Mount Sinai, *law* or *Torah* was understood as the sum total of God's disclosure of himself to his people. (*S/R*, 12.)

■ A team or committee might work out an arrangement of Psalms 19 as a choral reading. Prepare a script that two or more voices can read responsively, in unison, and as solo voices. Interesting contrasts may be achieved by using light, medium, and heavy voices. Modern versions of the Bible or hymns based on Psalms 19 (*The*

Methodist Hymnal, 43 and 365) might be used. A special group may be selected to present the psalm as a choral reading or the entire class may be assigned parts to read. Before or after the reading discuss: What affirmations does the psalm make about God? What view of the law is set forth? What is the response of the obedient servant to this law?

This brings us to an important conclusion: the source of Israel's faith was God's disclosure of himself to his people. At Mount Sinai God made an agreement with Israel that was based upon the revelation of himself contained in his law. The people received this revelation by committing themselves to a way of life governed by obedience to the law. Thus, through the agreement at Mount Sinai Israel gave herself to God as the only object worthy of her trust.

But this agreement at Mount Sinai was not made once by the generation living at that time and then forgotten. Recent study has shown that after the Israelites settled in Canaan they gathered at the shrine at Shechem every seven years to renew the agreement. It is probable that the material in Exodus, chapters 19 through 24 and 32 through 34, was read at these occasions every seven years.

Why would the people come together for this special worship every seven years? The answer: so that the people who made a pilgrimage could take part in a ceremony that made them partners in the Sinai agreement. There they heard the story again of how God had revealed himself to his people through Moses; they listened to the reading of the law and pledged themselves to live according to its demands; and thus, they experienced anew the trustworthiness of God which assured their well-being. (Read Deuteronomy 27:9-26; Psalms 51 and 81.)

This is the point where these chapters shed light upon our own relationship to God. Of course, we do not make pilgrimages to Shechem to renew our agreement with God. But we do gather regularly in our churches to celebrate God's disclosure of himself to us. There from time to time we listen to the reading of these narratives that report how God made an agreement with Israel at Mount Sinai. The reading is something more than a recollection of the events that happened to a group of nomads thousands of years ago. It is a way God makes us aware of his living presence; it is a way of God's including us in the agreement he made with Israel.

As we share in the agreement that God made with his people at Mount Sinai, the answers to questions about our faith begin to come clear. The source of *our* faith is God's disclosure of himself to us. Obviously, the agreement at Mount Sinai does not include all that God has revealed about himself, but it is an important part of that ongoing revelation upon which our faith is founded. The God of Mount Sinai is absolutely trustworthy.

■ Discover the context (setting) for Exodus 32 by reading the headings at the top of the columns in the Revised Standard Version, Exodus 19 through Numbers 10. List the most crucial events on chalkboard or newsprint. Locate these on the timeline (Resource Packet, item 5).

■ A research team, assigned in advance, may present reports on (1) The use and meaning of the word *covenant* as it appears at various places in the Bible. (See *S/R*, 11; *The Interpreter's Bible*, volume 1, pages 354-57; *The Interpreter's Dictionary of the Bible*; or other commentaries on the Bible.) (2) The place of the *Torah* in Hebrew history and its relation to the covenant. (See *S/R*, 12 and *The Interpreter's Bible*, volume I, pages 972 and 356, or you may wish to interview a rabbi.) Allow time for discussion of new ideas.

THE PEOPLE BREAK LOOSE

The people became restless and impatient when they "saw that Moses delayed to come down from the mountain" (Exodus 32:1a). They interpreted his prolonged absence as a sign that the God he served had deserted them.

Even as God was giving himself to the people through the law, they were turning away from him to worship other gods. Idolatry was not something that sprang up on the edges of Israel's religious experience. The people demanded other gods at the very moment when God was making an agreement with them that assured their well-being.

Why did they make that fatal choice? The answer seems to be fairly clear. The God who spoke to the people through Moses was beyond their control. He could not be *used* by the people. He cared for the people by giving himself to them, but he was not something they had made. He could not be ordered about, according to their will. He was totally different from them. He demanded that they turn away from themselves to follow him.

Here then is the age-old problem of the object of man's faith. The solution to the problem, which is narrated in Exodus 32, reveals how men turn from the true object of faith, the living God, to seek their security and well-being in the worship of idols. (*S/R,* 13.)

The completeness of Aaron's failure in this situation is emphasized by the fact that he made an altar before the calf and led the people in worshiping what they had made with their hands. On the next day they rose up early, "and offered burnt offerings and brought peace offerings; and the people sat down to eat and drink, and rose up to play" (Exodus 32:5-6) . (The phrase *rose up to play* is a Hebrew expression that refers to the sexual orgies which usually accompanied the worship of idols.)

Who was responsible for this corruption of the life of the people at the very time God was establishing a covenant relationship with them? (See Exodus 32:7-8.) The point is unmistakable. The people corrupted themselves. They had become so perverse that they ascribed their deliverance from Egypt to idols made by their own hands. Therefore, the Lord said to Moses, "I have seen this people, and behold, it is a stiff-necked people" (Exodus 32:9) .

"A stiff-necked people" is a vivid phrase that conveys the stubborn and rebellious spirit of the people. They chose a course that led them headlong toward destruction and ruin. Even Aaron, who had served faithfully with Moses, was swept along by the madness of the people; he became a partner of their idolatry.

IDOL WORSHIP TODAY

Our study of this passage requires that we use it to examine our own lives. We must seek honestly for signs of golden calves in our own situation. The place to look is not in the dark corners of our lives but at the center of our religious life.

One of the most important features of our religious life is the building where we gather to worship God. Properly used a church building is a symbol of the reality of God in our lives and an effective means of keeping our faith strong and vital. But all too often the building becomes an end in itself and is made an object of faith that replaces the living God. (S/R, 14.) Several years ago I attended a congregational meeting to consider an imaginative and creative proposal for changing the chancel and nave of the building. The proposal was voted down not because of careful consideration of its strengths and weaknesses but simply because the majority of the congregation refused to consider it. As people spoke against the proposal, the reason given over and over again was that they couldn't worship if anything were changed in the building. Why do men turn from God to worship the work of their own hands?

Another idolatrous tendency in our religious life is manifested in our attitude toward the Bible. (S/R, 15.) The biblical literature is the faithful witness of men who experienced the reality of God in their lives. When the Bible is used to help men become aware of and responsive to the presence and power of God in human history, it is an ally of faith. But this requires that the Bible be read and understood. (*S/R*, 16.) New translations of the Bible, such as the Revised Standard Version and the New English Bible, are produced from time to time so that modern men may read the Scriptures in language which is up-to-date and easily understood. These translations are often opposed and attacked not on the basis of scholarly consideration of their merits but because they represent a departure from the familiar language of some older version. Those who take this position have turned from the God who reveals himself through the Bible to worship the words of the Bible.

Why do men choose to put their trust in a book rather than in the living God? Is it because a book can be manipulated and controlled so that it becomes a means for securing approval for that which men want? But God is not the Bible. The living God who speaks to men through the Bible cannot be used by men. (*S/R*, 17.)

As we search our religious life in the light of this passage of Scripture, we must not overlook our tendency to idolize our nation. There are signs throughout the land that the real object of our religious devotion is the nation.

■ Divide the class into five groups. Let each group discuss one of the following questions: How are you included in the agreement that God made with Israel? How does man today look for a God whom he can control and use for his own purpose? What idols do we use to justify our own immoral acts? How might each of the following become an idol: (1) the church—*S/R*, 14, (2) the Bible —*S/R*, 15, (3) the nation—*S/R*, 13? What evidence is there that America, like Israel of old, assumes that the relationship between her and God is automatic and permanent? Share your ideas with the group.

■ Or divide the group into teams of three persons. Each team will write a description of an event in modern life that parallels the golden calf incident. Read the descriptions aloud. (See *S/R*, 18.)

37

GOD VISITS THEIR SIN UPON THEM

The sin of Aaron and the people was all the more terrible because it was a rejection of the central event of Israel's faith. The people had forsaken the living God and had credited their deliverance from Egypt to the gods represented by the golden calf. The horrible result of their backsliding was the disruption of the agreement in which they received their salvation. Even Joshua and Moses, the great mediators of the covenant, were turned against them. Moses, who had delivered them from Egypt, was transformed into a rod of wrath: "Moses' anger burned hot, and he threw the tables out of his hands and broke them at the foot of the mountain" (Exodus 32:19b).

Israel stood condemned before God and his judgment of her was inevitable. Not even Moses could resolve the conflict and turn back the punishment that the people had brought upon themselves. He attempted to atone for the sins of the people, "but the LORD said to Moses, 'Whoever has sinned against me, him will I blot out of my book'" (Exodus 32: 33). The gift of the covenant was life, but the payment for disobedience was death. According to this narrative, the agreement between God and Israel was not automatic and permanent. It was a gift of God that demanded a faithful response from the people. When the people turned away and placed their faith in the gods whom they had made, they chose death and destruction.

This passage speaks clearly and powerfully to our present situation. When we turn from the living God to worship other gods, we corrupt ourselves. Only one object is supremely worthy of our faith: the living God. If we place our faith in any other person or thing, whatever we worship destroys us.

Our situation today is extremely perilous. The confusion and frustration that we experience individually and collectively threaten to overwhelm us. In this situation we cannot save ourselves. Only God can save us. But God seems to many of us to be remote and unconcerned with our needs. We are tempted to seek an assurance and safety that is more immediate and visible than the saving presence of the living God. So we are faced with a choice between the true peace of faith in God and the false peace of trust in the gods we imagine in our hearts and make with our hands. The ruin and destruction in our lives are evidence that we have made the incredible choice: we have made for ourselves a molten calf, and have worshiped it and sacrificed it. Therefore, in the day when God visits us, he visits our sin upon us.

Because we are a stiff-necked people, the God who seeks us in love must always come to us as our judge. The conflict that rages within and without is not an evidence that God has left us but a sign that he is with us as our judge. The agreement that assured our well-being is broken. Our realization of what has happened is often delayed until some moment of shattering self-understanding. Then we see that the Lord is judging us, because we made the calf.

■ The leadership team will display pictures clipped from the front page of this week's newspapers. On the basis of the biblical interpretation and this chapter's interpretation of it, how do you understand judgment? Would you interpret the events pictured as signs of God's judgment? Why or why not? How can judgment and punishment be an expression of God's *saving* presence?
■ Pray together the Prayer of Confession 724, *The Methodist Hymnal.*
■ Let the leadership team be prepared to make assignments for the next chapter of study and the members of the group be prepared to accept the assignments.

YOU ONLY HAVE I KNOWN

All of us have some general knowledge of human nature. We are familiar with statements that begin with words like *man is* or *mankind is* or *humanity is.* These statements are important because they convey certain generalizations about the bases of our social relationships. For example, we say that man is a thinking animal and this statement becomes the underlying assumption of much that we do in the field of education, communication, and entertainment.

But there is another kind of knowledge of human nature that is quite different from these generalizations. This other kind of knowledge is usually introduced by assertions that begin with words like *John is, my wife is, my parents are, my*

■ *As you arrive at your place of meeting, check the assignment chart for specific preparation to be made before the session begins.*

■ Set goals for your study of this chapter as suggested on page 17.

41

partner has, and so forth. This kind of knowledge of human nature is intimate, personal, and particular.

Obviously, our life together requires that we make generalizations about human nature. Without generalizations we could have no psychology, sociology, or political science. We could have no practice of law or medicine, no teaching or counseling. But it is also obvious that our life together would be barren and empty without intimate, personal, and particular knowledge of each other. Without the intimate and particular experience of each other, we could have no love, no hatred, no laughter, no sorrow, no hope, no despair, no loyalty, no betrayal. In short, we would be deprived of all those experiences that are signs of our true humanity.

The reason for this discussion of how we experience intimate, personal, and particular knowledge of each other is that it closely parallels the relationship between God and Israel which is central to the Scripture we are studying in this chapter. The word that the Lord spoke to the people of Israel as recorded in Chapter 3 of Amos begins with a statement about knowledge: "You only have I known of all the families of the earth" (Amos 3:2*a*).

The knowledge of God contained in Amos 3 is not general information about God. Instead it is the witness of a man (Amos) who had experienced an intimate, personal, and particular relationship with God. God had chosen and known his people Israel in a way that was different from his relationship with "all the families of the earth."

We must press one step farther the parallel between our personal knowledge of each other and Israel's knowledge of God. The basic assumption of Amos 3 is that Israel's responsibility to God rested squarely upon her intimate relationship with God. Just as our personal experience of another person carries with it the obligation to care for that person, so Israel's knowledge of God carried with it the obligation to trust, honor, and obey him. Amos proclaimed that

42

Israel had failed to meet the demands of knowing God and had exposed her life to his judgment. Because she had neglected the responsibilities of her particular experience of God, the privilege of that experience had become the occasion for her punishment. Thus, the gracious, self-giving words of revelation are joined to a stern prediction of judgment in a verse that provides the theme for all of Amos 3.

> "You only have I known
> of all the families of the earth;
> therefore I will punish you
> for all your iniquities"
>
> (Amos 3:2).

■ Look at the filmslip "Getting Inside the Bible," using Script Two (Resource Packet, item 1). The Leaders' Guide in the packet contains suggestions for its use.

■ In four small groups of four to six persons, engage in a study of Amos 3, using the method described on the chart "Study a Portion of the Bible" (Resource Packet, item 2, procedure 2 or 3). See the Leaders' Guide in the packet.

■ On chalkboard or newsprint, list the main ways in which Israel had failed to meet the demands of knowing God. Beside this list, make another list of the ways Christians fail to meet these demands. Do you believe we are in danger of a similar judgment? What can we do, if anything?

THE LORD HAS DONE IT

As we begin this study of Amos 3 it is important to observe that here for the first time in the Old Testament we are dealing with material written by an author whom we can identify. What do we know about Amos? We know that his ministry probably lasted a very short time during the reign of Jeroboam II, who was king of Israel from about 787-747 B.C. (Amos 1:1). Although he was a native of Tekoa, a fortified town in the southern kingdom of Judah, the ministry of Amos was carried out in the northern kingdom and centered in the great shrine at Bethel (Amos 1:1; 7:10-15). There is also evidence that Amos prophesied during the last years of Jeroboam's rule when it appeared that Assyria would overrun Israel and carry the people "into exile beyond Damascus" (Amos 5:27a). Thus, his ministry lasted for a brief period, sometime between 750 and 747 B.C.

The most important fact about the Book of Amos is given in 1:1: "Hear this word that the Lord has spoken against you, O people of Israel, against the whole family which I brought up out of the land of Egypt." In these words the prophet identified the people to whom he spoke. He identified them as a people who had experienced deliverance from Egypt through the power of the living God. Amos did not stand outside that experience but was a part of it. He too was one of those who had been delivered, not historically but by faith. His whole ministry was founded upon the faith that had been inspired by what God had done for his people. (S/R, 19.) The point is simply this: Amos was nurtured in the faith of Israel, and all that he said and did must be understood as an expression of that faith.

Thus, Amos began his message in this chapter with an affirmation familiar to every Israelite: God has called Israel out of Egypt and has established a unique relationship with her. In this relationship Israel had experienced an immediate knowledge of God that was comparable to the intimate communion of husband and wife in marriage.

During the time of Amos the people assumed that because God had dealt graciously with his people in the past he would protect them from all their enemies in the present and in the future. The prosperity of the land gave support to the idea that God would never forsake his people. Assyria had defeated Syria but had not been powerful enough to follow up with an invasion of Israel.

The nation had seized the opportunity to restore her commerce and in time had entered on a period of great prosperity. All of this new-found splendor was popularly acclaimed as a sign of God's special favor. The shrines were crowded by people offering sacrifices to God.

When Amos went north to the royal shrine at Bethel about 750 B.C., he saw all of this (Amos 7:10-15). What he saw led him to a conclusion radically different from that which was celebrated by the people at the king's sanctuary. As we have noted, he shared with his contemporaries the conviction that God had called Israel into a special relationship. However, for him that relationship did not guarantee Israel's well-being in the present and in the future. Instead, that relationship, which the people mistakenly found so comforting, was the basis for a disaster soon to come:

> "Therefore I will punish you
> for all your iniquities"
> (Amos 3:2).

GOD'S RELATIONSHIP TO US

These observations about the foundation of Amos' ministry in the covenant that God made with Israel may seem far removed from our present situation. Yet if we reflect upon them seriously, we may discover that they are not as remote as they appear. For example, just as Amos was prepared for his prophetic ministry by full participation in the religious heritage of his people, so we are prepared for our own service by sharing in the rich resources of our faith. (S/R, 20.) Surely God has a purpose for each one of us just as he had a purpose for Amos of Tekoa. But we do not become responsive and sensitive to God's purpose for us as individuals in isolation from what God has done for his people in the past. One of the reasons for our studying the Bible together is that through its witness we may receive the kind of personal knowledge about God that Amos experienced.

We also participate in our religious heritage when we worship together in our churches. We gather for prayers,

45

praise, preaching, and ritual. In these acts we acknowledge that God has given himself to us in particular events of our history, such as the creation of the church. The most important single factor in understanding our life together in the church is the faith that God's relationship with us has inspired. We must not allow our worship of God in our churches to degenerate into an assembly where we congratulate ourselves on having God on our side.

■ Read silently *S/R,* 19 and 20. Then in small groups discuss these questions: (1) In light of the paragraph above, how does my feeling about worship influence my attendance at worship services of this congregation? (2) How can worship help me see any connection between the Bible and the important questions I face or the ethical decisions I must make?

Today we live in a period of unprecedented national prosperity. How are we to interpret this prosperity? We are tempted to see it as a sign that God who has blessed us in the past will always be with us to preserve us and protect us from our foes. The logic of this interpretation goes like this: "We have more of the good things of life than other people; we have these good things because God is on our side; and, therefore, we will never be defeated." *(S/R,* 21.)

Amos compels us to consider *another* interpretation of our prosperity. If we follow his leadership, then we are helped to see that the good things we enjoy are gifts of God's mercy. We are sustained by his unmerited goodness toward us. To forget this is to turn our back on the living God and to destroy our relationship with him. In periods of national prosperity we are always in danger of putting our trust in possessions.

The disaster that Amos predicted for Israel was not the result of blind fate or historical accident but the work of God himself. Amos' participation in the religious heritage of his people had taught him to look for evidences of God's activity in what was taking place in the life of the nation. In Amos 3:3-6a the prophet has raised a series of rhetorical questions. In each case the expected answer was "no." The basis of each question was a commonplace observation about cause and effect. For instance, he asked:

> Does a lion roar in the forest,
> when he has no prey?
> (Amos 3:4*a*) .

The obvious answer was "no." But Amos did not string together this series of rhetorical questions in order to emphasize the obvious. He used this literary device to underscore for his hearers and readers the fact that the punishment which was about to come upon Israel did not lie outside God's relationship to his people but originated in that relationship. The climax came when he asked:

> Does evil befall a city,
> unless the LORD has done it?
> (Amos 3:6*b*) .

The intended answer was "no." But that was not obvious. To establish the cause and effect relationship between Israel's impending doom and the God who knew her in the covenant was the primary task of the prophet's ministry. That was what "the Lord God showed" him in the life of the people and that was what determined the content of his message from God to Israel (read Amos 7:1-9; 8:1-3).

SIGNS OF THE TIMES

Once more we may follow the lead of the prophet as we attempt to read the signs of our own times. (*S/R,* 22.) No one would question the fact that evils have befallen this nation. Nor would one question the fact that we as a people may be overtaken by greater evil than we have heretofore experienced. But are we ready to interpret the evil we fear as the result of God's righteous judgment? We are quite content to proclaim his judgment upon other people. We do

47

not accept the fact that there is a cause and effect relationship between the evil we experience and his punishing us
for our iniquities. For example, our cities are torn by race
riots, but we dismiss them as communist plots. Is it possible
that these are the judgment of God? A president is assassinat-
ed, but we explain it away as human action. Could this be
the judgment of God upon the nation? Thousands of our
people are deprived of the necessities of life. Some Christians
condemn their *supposed* lack of initiative and call it God's
judgment upon them. (*S/R, 23.*) In reality, rioting and other
signs of their discontent may be God's judgment on the
whole society that allows injustice. The question cannot be
evaded.

■ Plan a panel discussion on these questions: (1) Do we in this
country act as if our prosperity is a sign of God's favor? If so,
how? (What are the implications of such songs as "God Bless
America"?) (2) How do we take signs of God's past favors as
guarantees of our future well-being? (3) In what ways do we let
justice stop at our national boundaries? *S/R,* 21, 22, and 23 will
provide some stimulating ideas. Follow the panel by reactions of
three kinds from the group: (1) reactions to the points made by
the panelists; (2) reactions to the evidence given to support their
conclusions; (3) reactions as to the meaning of the panelists' conclusions for our country's future.
■ According to the biblical views, God acts in history. See *S/R,*
22, Romans 1:16-32, Amos 9:7-8, and Hebrews 11. Do you believe
God is acting today? How? Especially do you think God works in
ways that include human responsibility? If so, what do you see as
your specific local responsibility, in the light of your study of this
unit so far?

In the events that were occurring during his own day Amos
heard God speaking as he had spoken at the exodus from
Egypt, at the covenant making at Mount Sinai, and at the
conquest of Canaan. God's power was not confined to the
past but was released in the present. Amos was called to
witness to the fact in his own acts and words. Therefore, his
words were God's Word in the sense that his human re-

sponse was the agency through which God revealed himself
in the crisis of Jeroboam's reign.

So although Amos must be interpreted within the framework of Israel's historical faith, there is a quality in his ministry that breaks with everything in Israel's past. He himself
refused to be tagged with a neat label from the past (read
Amos 7:14). God revealed himself to Amos and the shepherd
of Tekoa was torn out of his previous existence and set in an
entirely new situation. "The Lord took me from following
the flock, and the Lord said to me, 'Go, prophesy to my people Israel'" (Amos 7:15). Faithfulness to the God who took
him and spoke to him required that he give up everything
except dependence upon God alone. And in this dependence
upon God he found a new freedom which released him from
the routine religious practices.

We are studying the Bible, perhaps the most important
part of our religious heritage. But our study is not directed
toward the Bible as an end in itself. Rather, our purpose is
to hear the living God who speaks to us through the witness
of the Bible. We are studying this chapter from the Book
of Amos not because we worship Amos but because Amos'
witness helps us to hear and respond to what God is saying
to us in our time, through our lives. The word that God
would have proclaimed in our time will not be heard unless
he can find faithful messengers who will identify themselves
with the source of their message and speak as if God himself
were heard through their lips. It is a fearful thing to speak
God's message, but we must do it.

Through our religious heritage we have been made aware
of God's presence in our lives. But our ultimate allegiance
is not to that heritage. Our loyalty is claimed by the living
God who is not confined to our heritage. His Word sets us
free from the past to serve him now in the present. We honor
our past, not by slavish devotion to it, but by discerning in it

49

the presence and the power of the God who even now is at work in our lives preparing us to become his witnesses. Our understanding of the biblical witness is shallow and superficial unless it helps us to see that faithfulness to God requires that we must be willing to break with everything in our past if necessary and give up everything except dependence upon God alone. (S/R, 24.)

■ Have seated in a circle in the midst of the group four or five members previously recruited and prepared by reading S/R, 17 and 24, and Philippians 3:12-16. They react to this statement in terms of their responsibilities (including homemaking): "Faithfulness to God requires that we must be willing to break with everything in our past if necessary and give up everything except dependence upon God alone." Does this mean that we are to break with everything in our past in the sense of forgetting it, disregarding it, despising it, or treating it lightly? If none of these, what then? What do we do when we "break with our past"? How do we *relate* to the past in faith?

THEY DO NOT KNOW HOW TO DO RIGHT

Amos' immediate sense of the reality of God's presence in his own life was the basis for his appraisal of the great tumults and oppressions within Israel (Amos 3:9b). His protest against "those who store up violence and robbery in their strongholds" was based upon his awareness of God's demand for justice and righteousness in the present (Amos 3:10b). Amos understood that the God of Mount Sinai was the God of Israel. Therefore, Israel's welfare required that the people honor God by doing what was right in the whole sweep of life.

On what ground did Amos conclude that Israel did "not know how to do right"? The basis for his judgment was the law that God had given at Mount Sinai. Recent research has shown that the specific sins condemned as "violence and robbery" were acts prohibited by the law contained in Exodus 23:1-9. Amos did not mention the law. He assumed that it was well known in Israel and that the people could not be excused for breaking it. The problem was not that the people were ignorant of the law but rather that they openly disobeyed the law. To Amos this was more than a crime against humanity. It was sin against God.

Amos' appraisal of the situation of Israel in 750 B.C. compels us to take a hard look at affairs in our nation at this particular time. In our pledge of allegiance to the flag we declare that this nation is "under God." This is a kind of formal acknowledgment that all our affairs must be submitted to the sovereign power of God, that nothing in our lives is outside his rule. But our deeds do not conform to our profession. "The great tumults within her,/and the oppressions in her midst" have made this nation an object of scorn and ridicule for many of the people of the earth. Our problem is simply that we as a people have chosen to "store up violence and robbery" in our strongholds. (S/R, 25.)

Our study of this chapter from the Book of Amos requires that we face squarely every attempt to limit the power of God to the boundaries of our own nation. The fact that we do not conduct our affairs as a nation "under God" does not mean that we are really not "under God." It simply means that God's reign which is offered to us as the source of our true peace and well-being must now be our inescapable judgment. We are also challenged by Amos to acknowledge that our particular and personal experience of God's presence does not exhaust the reality of his judging and redeeming presence in the world. Our reluctance to affirm God's rule in Russia and eastern Europe and in China may be something more than a failure to analyze the international situation. It may also be a sign that we are deaf to the words that the Lord God is speaking to us. If we have not seen his presence *everywhere*, we may not have seen him *anywhere*.

THE GREAT HOUSES SHALL COME TO AN END

Amos saw no evidence that the people would heed his message and seek their good in faithfulness to God. Therefore, he concluded that nothing could save them from the ruin of their evil ways. The picture he painted of the future was absolute destruction. "As the shepherd rescues from the mouth of the lion two legs, or a piece of an ear, so shall the people of Israel who dwell in Samaria be rescued, with the corner of a couch and a part of a bed" (Amos 3:12). He did not suggest that a remnant of Israel would be spared. Two legs and a piece of an ear snatched from the mouth of a marauding lion were symbols of the utter devastation that Israel would experience at the hands of the invading Assyrians. All that would be left in Israel (the northern kingdom) was the ruin of her former glory.

How can we relate Amos' message of unrelieved doom to our contemporary situation? His message is certainly not one that we can easily accept nor is it one that we would readily proclaim. But perhaps our natural resistance to his ministry is a sign of how much we need it. In the face of a soaring crime rate, with an increase in "violence and robbery" as in Amos' day, do you believe we face destruction and ruin? Amos says his nation is going to suffer for the wrongdoing of the wealthy. Could it happen here?

The last strongholds of resistance to the word of God's judgment in our society are often our houses of worship and our comfortable dwelling places. All too often the praise and thanksgiving that we offer to God in our churches are cheap substitutes for repentance and reform in all our affairs. Certainly there is nothing wrong with worship in itself. But worship that does not help us to live according to God's laws is an offense to God. It lulls us into a sense of false peace and blinds us to the disaster that is about to overtake us. Amos reminds us that even our houses of worship will be subject to God's judgment when he punishes us.

During the last few years the struggle to secure civil rights for all Americans has forced us to consider the right of every citizen to live in any neighborhood where he can afford the housing. (*S/R,* 26.) The antagonisms have revealed that now as in the time of Amos the real center of our religious life is not the altar but the hearth. The slogan *a man's home is his castle* has been used to defeat fair housing legislation and to deny minority groups equal opportunity to choose where they will live. It is sometimes said (without foundation in fact) that real estate values decline when a nonwhite family moves into a white neighborhood. Does this line of reasoning suggest that our faith is in our property? Is our god our own imagined advantage? In order to promote our own interests are we willing to sacrifice justice and mercy and equality on the altar of our greed?

■ Let the group pretend they are a resolutions committee, meeting at the next General Conference. Formulate a resolution on housing for the new *Discipline,* basing it on your understanding of Amos' word as God's spokesman. (For examples of resolutions, see *Doctrines and Discipline of The Methodist Church,* 1964, paragraphs 1821-1826) . See S/R, 26 as factual background material.

■ Worship by presenting several "words from the world" and "words from the Lord" in clippings from today's paper. These may present problems, stories of need, opportunities for service, and so on. *S/R,* 25 might open this period. As these "words" are read, let everyone look at the picture on page 176 in this book.

■ Let the leadership team be prepared to make assignments for the next chapter of study and the members to accept them.

What one generation hears God speak through a particular symbol is not necessarily what another generation will hear through that symbol.

4

HIS NAME SHALL BE CALLED EMMANUEL

Our study of Genesis 2:4b–3:24, Exodus 32, and Amos 3 has helped us to see how Israel's unfaithfulness broke the relationship that God had established with her and exposed her to his judgment and punishment. We have seen this as a tragic development in the history of Israel as well as a penetrating insight into our own situation.

One of the purposes of our study of the Old Testament in the church is to help us to see how the gracious acts of God are rejected over and over again by a stiff-necked idolatrous people. As we have reflected together upon the meaning of this repeated rejection of God by those whom he has loved and cherished, we have been forced to admit that we are not

■ *As you arrive at your place of meeting, check the assignment chart for specific preparation to be made before the session begins.*

■ Set goals for your study of this chapter as suggested on page 17.

innocent spectators. The events that took place in the garden of Eden, at Mount Sinai, and at Bethel were not just isolated acts in the experience of Israel. They are also acts of rebellion against God in which we all participate and for which we all are responsible.

But how may this bad news about us be reconciled to the claim that the Bible is a witness to the good news? We have already suggested that the bad news about our unfaithfulness may be interpreted as a necessary part of the good news about God. The experience of God's judgment in our lives is not evidence that God has rejected us. Instead, it is a sign that God will not leave us to die in our unfaithfulness. God punishes us because he seeks to lead us from unfaithfulness and death into faithfulness and life. The bad news about us is a part of God's redemptive work in our lives. The good news is simply that God knows our condition and has acted decisively and powerfully to fulfill his purposes in our lives.

What does God do to conquer the unfaithfulness in our lives? The answer of the biblical witness to this question is clear and unmistakable: God loves us absolutely and without condition. For those of us who share the Christian faith, the most complete expression of God's love for unfaithful men is the life, death, and resurrection of Jesus of Nazareth. God's purpose to create a faithful people, which is affirmed in the Old Testament, is made good in the events that are proclaimed in the New Testament. The relationship between the Old Testament and the New is not something that we impose upon two unrelated collections of literature. The relationship is one that we can discover as we recognize the power and presence of the living God leading us from unfaith to faith, from death to life, from narrow exclusivism to a faith for *all* men of all nations. (*S/R, 27.*)

■ Form groups of four or five persons. Share with your group the most important crisis through which you have ever passed. Did you experience a sense of God's presence or a power beyond yourself that helped you through the crisis or led you from unfaith to faith? Describe any ways in which you were changed.

IN THIS WAY

The narrative in the Gospel of Matthew of the birth of Jesus was written years after his death and resurrection. It must be read not as an eyewitness report but as a faithful attempt by the author of the Gospel of Matthew to proclaim what he and his fellow believers had experienced in the life, death, and resurrection of Jesus of Nazareth.

When Matthew was written (about A.D. 85), Palestine was occupied by Roman soldiers, the temple in Jerusalem had been destroyed, and Jesus had been rejected long before by the Jewish leaders and crucified by the Roman authorities. But for the author of Matthew the course of history had been reversed by what God had done in Jesus. God's purpose to create a faithful people had been realized at the very place where the unfaithfulness of men was expressed most tragically, at Calvary.

The sin of men reached a climax in the crucifixion of Jesus, but the last word was not man's sin but God's will to save. Jesus had been raised from the dead. He was present in the church through the power of the Holy Spirit. Therefore, the event that is reported in Matthew 1:18-25 is not just the birth of an infant, but it is also the experience of the risen Lord. The words "now the birth of Jesus Christ took place in this way" (Matthew 1:18a) do not introduce the biography of Jesus. Instead, they prepare us for hearing the church confess her Easter faith. The narrative of the birth appears in the Gospel of Matthew because in the resurrection of Jesus God had made good his purpose to conquer unfaithfulness by triumphing over death itself. The birth account tells us something about God's purpose.

Without the resurrection of Jesus there is no good news;

57

there is only the frustration of God's purpose by unfaithful men and the final defeat of the grave. So as we study this passage together our major task is to listen for the good news of God's victory and to share the author's faith in the risen Lord.

What the author of Matthew proclaimed about the risen Lord in this narrative was rooted and grounded in the life and death of Jesus of Nazareth. (*S/R*, 28 and 29.) This is an essential thing for us to keep in mind as we seek to interpret our own experience of the risen Lord. The good news we proclaim about the victory of God over death and unfaithfulness is not based upon speculation but upon the life of one who entered history as we do and who experienced the same limitations of human existence.

Thus in light of the Easter faith of the church the author of Matthew proclaimed those things in the life of Jesus of Nazareth that were most important. He began by declaring that from the very beginning of Jesus' life in his mother's womb he had been an expression of the power and presence of God. The author was a Jew and was fully acquainted with the Old Testament. Quite naturally Old Testament ideas and images most understandably conveyed his own thoughts. One of the usual ways for an Old Testament writer to say that the power and presence of the Lord was active in an individual was to say that the Spirit of the Lord had been given to him. In the early days of Israel's history her leaders were characteristically Spirit-endowed men and women, but from the exile on the Spirit was less evident in the life of the people. One of the ardent hopes in the Judaism of the first century was that God would send his Spirit upon his people and give them once again an immediate experience of his power and presence. (*S/R*, 30.)

In reflecting on the meaning and purpose of the life, death, and resurrection of Jesus, Matthew had been convinced that what had happened could not be explained or understood on the human plane alone. It had to be ascribed to the immediate and powerful presence of God himself. So he wrote, "When his mother Mary had been betrothed to Joseph, before they came together she was found to be with child of the Holy Spirit; and her husband Joseph, being a just man and unwilling to put her to shame, resolved to divorce her quietly" (Matthew 1:18*b* 19).

When we use the Apostles' Creed to affirm our faith, we say, "I believe . . . in Jesus Christ . . . who was conceived by the Holy Spirit."

What does this mean? It means that nothing less than the power and the presence of God himself is experienced in the life, death, and resurrection of Jesus. In Jesus the power of God is made available for our needs; in him the presence of God claims our absolute trust and obedience. The idea of conception by the Holy Spirit does not commit us to any particular theory of *how* the life of Jesus began. It does, however, express the fact that in the *totality* of his earthly existence we see revealed the fullness of God's power and presence.

■ What does it mean to be truly human? On newsprint or chalkboard make a list of characteristics of humanness, such as limited knowledge of the future or fear of the unknown. In the light of your list, the preceding paragraphs in this book, and *S/R*, 28 and 29, how is it good news that Jesus was fully human—that he entered history as we do and experienced the same limitations? Let one person read aloud S/R, 31. How does it affirm the idea that in Jesus we see revealed the power and presence of God?

The author of Matthew went on in this narrative to state how one arrived at this kind of faith in Jesus. He did this with dramatic skill by contrasting Joseph's initial rejection of Mary and her child to his final acceptance of them according to the commandment of God. "Her husband Joseph, being a just man and unwilling to put her to shame, resolved to divorce her quietly" (Mathew 1:19). This is a frank statement of how completely inadequate ordinary human wisdom had been when it attempted to make a judgment about the life of Jesus. (*S/R*, 31.) Joseph could not discern the power and presence of God in this event. The faith of the church was hidden from him until God enabled him to see.

> But as he considered this, behold, an angel of the Lord appeared to him in a dream, saying, "Joseph, son of David, do not fear to take Mary your wife, for that which is conceived in her is of the Holy Spirit; she will bear a son, and you shall call his name Jesus, for he will save his people from their sins" (Matthew 1:20-21).

The "angel of the Lord" was a familiar expression among the Jews. It was the instrument whereby God made himself known to men. The event of revelation customarily took place during a dream. Here the author declared that what human wisdom could never discover about Jesus had been disclosed to Joseph by an act of God.

At the conclusion of the narrative the result of what God revealed to him was expressed in his faithful obedience. "When Joseph woke from sleep, he did as the angel of the Lord commanded him; he took his wife, but knew her not until she had borne a son; and he called his name Jesus" (Matthew 1:24-25).

Again this narrative speaks to our own condition. It is true that none of us on the strength of our own wisdom can arrive at a faithful understanding of the life, death, and resurrection of Jesus. But this does not mean that our situation is hopeless. The good news that the author of Matthew proclaims in these verses about Joseph's pilgrimage from unfaith to faith is that God does not leave us to perish in our blindness. He comes to cure our blindness so that we might behold the reality of his power and presence in our lives.

■ Compare Joseph's pilgrimage from unfaith to faith with that of the man born blind (John 9:13-41). How were their experiences similar? Different? In what ways are we also blind? Are there times when we choose to remain blind to reality? When? Why? What are the causes of our spiritual blindness? Discuss the meaning of verses 39-41. Consult *The Interpreter's Bible,* volume 8, pages 619-20. In what way does Jesus pronounce judgment but at the same time not condemn honest doubt?

TO FULFILL WHAT THE LORD HAD SPOKEN

In our study of this passage up to this point we have ignored verses 22 and 23. We have left them for consideration here, because they are not essential to the development of the story and because they are used to give a summarizing interpretation of what has gone before: "All this took place to fulfill what the Lord had spoken by the prophet" (Matthew 1:22). Obviously, the writer had in mind some Old Testament prophecy that had been fulfilled in the way the birth of Jesus took place. Can we identify this prophecy and see how it was fulfilled in the birth of Jesus? (*S/R,* 32.)

If your Bible contains cross references or notes, you will see immediately that the verse quoted in Matthew 1:23 comes from Isaiah 7:14. Comparison of the two verses in the Revised Standard Version will show that the only noticeable difference is the use of the word *virgin* in Matthew instead of the word *young woman* as in Isaiah. This is really not a major difference. The Hebrew for "young woman" in Isaiah 7:14 is debatable and could possibly mean "virgin." Moreover, the quotation in Matthew 1:23 is not directly from the Hebrew, but from the Greek translation of the Hebrew Bible (our Old Testament), the Septuagint. The Greek for "virgin" in Matthew 1:23 is also debatable and could possibly mean "young woman." The point is that very little can be discovered by studying the derivations of these two different translations. If we want to find out why the author of Matthew quoted Isaiah 7:14, we will have to approach the matter in a different way. (*S/R,* 33 and 34.)

Let us begin by examining Isaiah 7:14 in its historical con-

text. The setting is fairly clear. Judah during the reign of
King Ahaz was sorely pressed by the combined armies of
Syria and Israel (the northern kingdom), who were trying
to force her (Judah) into a military alliance against Assyria.
During this period of national crisis (probably the year 734
B.C.) Isaiah of Jerusalem advised King Ahaz against seeking the security of his country through any kind of military
alliance. Instead, Isaiah urged the king to refuse to enter
the alliance and to seek the security of his kingdom by
strengthening his faith in God. He said to the king,

> "If you will not believe,
> surely you shall not be established"
> (Isaiah 7:9b).

But King Ahaz was not convinced of the wisdom of Isaiah's
counsel. Isaiah sensed that the king was about to choose a
course which would lead eventually to the destruction of the
kingdom. So in a last, desperate attempt to persuade the
king he asked him to seek a sign from the Lord that would
disclose the wisdom of trusting God instead of military alliance. The king refused, declaring that it was wrong to put
God to the test.

Isaiah saw through Ahaz' false piety and concluded that
he had determined to seek the security of his kingdom
through political maneuvering, regardless of what God might
do. Therefore, the prophet stopped trying to advise the king
and proclaimed that the Lord himself would give a sign
which would reveal the foolishness of the king's policy (Isaiah
7:10-14a).

The sign that Isaiah predicted was not a supernatural event
but the defeat of the armies of Israel and Syria by an invading army.

> "Behold, a young woman shall conceive and bear a son, and
> shall call his name Immanuel. . . . For before the child knows

how to refuse the evil and choose the good, the land before whose two kings you are in dread will be deserted. The LORD will bring upon you and upon your people and upon your father's house such days as have not come since the day that Ephraim departed from Judah—the king of Assyria" (Isaiah 7:14b-17).

The events that Isaiah foresaw on the international scene were interpreted by him as acts of God. Even the all-conquering Assyrians were subject to the Lord God and instruments of his purpose.

What is the relationship of the name *Immanuel* to this sign of God's judgment? The primary purpose of the passage in which the name appears is to state that the sign will occur in the immediate future (Isaiah 7:14b-16). The predicted sign was neither the birth of a son nor his being named Immanuel. The sign was the destruction that would be carried out in Palestine by the invaders. The birth and naming of the child were mentioned to emphasize that before an infant born in 734 B.C. had reached the age of moral distinction God would be with Ahaz and all his people, not giving them ease and prosperity but creating havoc among them because of their unfaithfulness. The king could deny God; he could turn away from God's messenger; but one thing he could not do: escape God's presence.

The name *Immanuel* is a compound of two Hebrew words, *Immanu,* which means "with us," and *El,* which means "God." Hence, Immanuel means "God with us." But in this context the name was not a confession of God's *favorable* presence. On the contrary, it was a symbol that God would be with his unfaithful people as their righteous judge. Let me repeat: Isaiah was affirming that God would be with his people—not to bless them (as they expected) but to judge.

The context supports the conclusion that Isaiah referred to a child born in a perfectly natural way. The significance of the child was not his miraculous birth; the significance

63

was that when he reached the age of accountability Judah would be faced with a settling of her accounts with God. Isaiah 7:14 probably did not refer to the naming of a particular child by an identifiable mother. Instead, it emphasized the radical change that Judah's unfaithfulness had caused in her relationship to God. There was nothing unusual about the name *Immanuel*. But probably it had always been understood as a symbol of Judah's favored position in the presence of God.

Now, however, the prophet had poured new meaning into the name by associating it with Judah's impending destruction. Immanuel—"God with us"—was no longer a sign of God's protection; instead it had become a symbol of the destruction unleashed in the land by the sins of Ahaz and his people.

What is there in this passage from the Book of Isaiah that had not been fulfilled by the time Matthew was writing? This is the central issue in determining the relationship between Isaiah 7:14 and Matthew 1:23. There can be no doubt that for the author of Matthew the birth of Jesus was the fulfillment of "what the Lord had spoken by the prophet" (Matthew 1:22). The core of Isaiah's prediction that Assyria would sweep over Israel, Syria, and Judah was filled to overflowing. Syria and Israel were defeated, and, although Judah was spared total destruction, she lost her independence. Thus, we may conclude that the author of Matthew did not refer to the prediction of the destruction of Israel, Syria, and Judah when he spoke of Isaiah's unfulfilled word.

In Matthew 1:23 the focus of attention is not the word of impending judgment but the prediction of the birth and naming of a child. There on the edge of Isaiah's message to King Ahaz the author of Matthew had heard a word of the Lord which for him had been awaiting fulfillment until the birth of Jesus. Thus we see that the meaning of the name *Immanuel* was not determined for the author of Matthew by the word which God spoke through Isaiah to Ahaz. He has clearly pushed beyond what Isaiah had intended to say when he used the name.

If we are to grasp the full impact of Matthew 1:23, then we must follow the Gospel writer as he redefined the meaning of Immanuel. The determining factor in this new interpretation of the word which the Lord spoke through Isaiah was not what had happened in 734 B.C. but what had happened when God raised Jesus from the dead. From the point of view of his Easter faith the author looked back upon the whole tragic sweep of Israel's history and concluded that here at last God had made good his promise to be with his people. In the life, death, and resurrection of this man the name *Immanuel* was no longer a hope which had failed, but it was now a living presence. The promise "God with us" had been filled to overflowing by the experience of the risen Lord in the church. Therefore, the author of Matthew could write:

All this took place to fulfill what the Lord had spoken by the prophet:

"Behold, a virgin shall conceive and
    bear a son,
and his name shall be called Emmanuel"
        (Matthew 1:22-23).

There is an important method of biblical interpretation illustrated for us in the way the author of Matthew used the name *Immanuel* as a vehicle for confessing his faith in the risen Lord. If we can understand how Matthew used an earlier revelation from God in *his* "Bible" (our Old Testament), but reinterpreted it in light of his faith in the risen Lord, we shall have discovered a way by which we can understand how God may speak to *us* through the Bible.

First, Matthew revealed that he was aware of how God

had disclosed himself to his people in the past. The name *Immanuel* was a part of the rich religious heritage which had been transmitted to him by the faithful witness of men of old.

Second, Matthew demonstrated that what one generation had heard God speak through a particular symbol was not necessarily the word which another generation would hear through that symbol. The name *Immanuel* was used by Isaiah and the author of Matthew to convey messages that were radically different in content.

Finally, the author of Matthew showed that the most important factor in determining the content of Scripture was the presence of the risen Lord. The test of the writer's faithfulness was not how closely he conformed to the intent of Isaiah or how free he was to follow his own creative imagination but how obedient he was to the Spirit of the risen Lord.

The method is this: (1) we must understand how God has revealed himself in the past; (2) we must understand that the meaning of a symbol will change from generation to generation, according to the needs of each; (3) the presence of the risen Lord is the most important factor in understanding the content of the Bible.

In our own study of these passages of Scripture we are seeking to become aware of the rich resources of our faith; we are seeking to use our creative insights in applying the Scripture to our own situation. But in the last analysis the voice which we must hear as we study Scripture is not that of men of old nor that of our contemporary situation. The voice we must hear is that of one called Immanuel, "God with us."

■ Let one member of the leadership team or a member of the group be prepared to lead the class in a study of Matthew 1:22-23 as it is interpreted on pages 61-65 in this study book. Special attention should be given to: the relationship of Matthew 1:22-23 to Isaiah 7:14; the historical setting of Isaiah 7:14; the meaning of the name

Immanuel as used by Isaiah and by Matthew; the fulfillment of prophecy. *S/R*, 33 and 34 will be of help. Also *The Interpreter's Bible* and *The Interpreter's Dictionary of the Bible* are excellent sources of information.

Or the leader might use the chart "Study a Portion of the Bible" (Resource Packet, item 2) to direct the group in a study of Matthew 1:22-23. Specific directions for using the chart are given in the Leaders' Guide accompanying the packet.

GOD WITH US

We must spare no effort to see what a tremendous act of faith was required for the author of Matthew to apply the name *Immanuel* to Jesus. On the surface, everything that had happened pointed to God's absence rather than his presence. We have already mentioned the crucifixion of Jesus and the destruction of the temple as events which surely must have come as soul-shattering experiences to the writer of this passage.

We must also remember that the author was a Jew who was fully acquainted with the tragedy which Israel had experienced because of her rebellion against God. How could God really be with his people where they had experienced a whole series of disasters? This question is reflected again and again in the Old Testament, and it must certainly have been familiar to the author of Matthew. Perhaps the best way to appreciate the faith of this writer is to contrast his reaction to Israel's tragedy with other reactions found in the Old Testament.

The Preacher in the Book of Ecclesiastes illustrates a response to Israel's failure which was probably typical of many who could see nothing except repeated frustration in human history. The following words are an eloquent expression of the boredom of one resigned to experiencing the same old thing over and over again:

A generation goes, and a generation comes,
but the earth remains for ever,

The sun rises and the sun goes down,
   and hastens to the place where it rises.
The wind blows to the south,
   and goes round to the north;
round and round goes the wind,
   and on its circuit the wind returns.
All streams run to the sea,
   but the sea is not full;
to the place where the streams flow,
   there they flow again.
All things are full of weariness;
   a man cannot utter it;
the eye is not satisfied with seeing,
   nor the ear filled with hearing.
What has been is what will be,
   and what has been done is what will
     be done;
   and there is nothing new under the sun
                  (Ecclesiastes 1:4-9).

Not all persons were able to respond to God's apparent absence from human history with the bored resignation of the Preacher. There were others like Job who were angered by God's seeming withdrawal from the tragedy of human life. (See Job 24:1-3, 12.)

The author of Matthew 1:18-25 had looked the tragedy of Israel square in the face. He knew the full power of the Preacher's boredom and Job's anger. But something had happened that carried him beyond any of these reactions to Israel's tragedy. He had experienced the risen Lord. The question of God's presence in human experience had been raised in all its stark reality by the tragedy of the cross and the question had been answered by the power of the Resurrection. (*S/R*, 35 and 36.) God was present at the very place where he seemed absent, at the cross. He was present in power; and, through that power, the writer of this passage and all who were joined to him in the church had been brought from death to life, from unfaith to faith. What God had promised to Israel had been fulfilled. Therefore, the author of Matthew could make no more appropriate confession of his faith than to write:

All this took place to fulfill what the Lord had spoken by the prophet:

"Behold, a virgin shall conceive and
    bear a son,
and his name shall be called Emmanuel"
    (Matthew 1:22-23).

The use of the name *Immanuel* in itself is a sign that the author of Matthew had experienced the solution of the riddle of Israel's history. We have no reason to believe that it was an unusual name. But we have every reason to believe that the name had been associated with Israel's rebellion and failure, that "God with us" reminded the faithful Jew of disobedience, punishment, and judgment. However, for this writer, Immanuel—"God with us"—had become a symbol of the fact that God had acted so powerfully and conclusively in the life, death, and resurrection of Jesus that the rebellion and failure of the people had been overcome.

For him what God had done in Jesus Christ was so new, so decisive, and so triumphant that it answered the boredom of Ecclesiastes and silenced the anger of Job. In the ministry of Jesus, God had done a radically new thing; and, by faith, the author of Matthew had perceived God's purpose (read Isaiah 43:19). Therefore, when Matthew took the name *Immanuel* from the religious heritage of his people to interpret what God had done in Jesus Christ, he did not define Jesus according to the way that name had been used in the past. Instead, he redefined Immanuel in terms of the new experience of God's redemptive presence that Jesus had brought to his people. The proof of how successful he was is demonstrated by the fact that when we hear Immanuel today we do not think of the prophecy of destruction in Isaiah 7:14 but of the proclamation of the good news in

Matthew 1:23. Immanuel—"God with us." When we hear or speak it, it is our confession that in Jesus God is so redemptively present that even the havoc of our sins has been overcome.

Bruce Catton, a historian of the Civil War, has described how Abraham Lincoln unlocked the meaning of the battle of Gettysburg in his Gettysburg Address. What Catton wrote about Lincoln's words applies also to the witness of the author of Matthew:

> It was the queer fate of the men who fought over the great question of Union that this most desperate and spectacular of all their battles should not be entirely comprehensible until after all of the dead had been buried, the wounded tended, the field itself made into a park, and the armies gone far below the horizon, fighting other battles in other places. Then the President would come and speak a few sentences, and the deep meaning of the fight would at last begin to clear. Then the perplexing mists and shadows would fade and Gettysburg would reveal itself as a great height from which men could glimpse a vista extending far into the undiscovered future.*

Long after Jesus had lived, died, and been raised from the dead, the author of Matthew came and spoke the word *Immanuel,* and the deep meaning of the life of Jesus began to clear. The word drives the mists and shadows away and the risen Lord reveals himself as the center from which men of faith discern that God is indeed with us.

■ Let four or five persons, with one acting as moderator, discuss the following questions for about eight minutes while the remainder of the class listens. *S/R,* 35 and 36 would be helpful to the discussion. Throughout this chapter we have been reading about "experiencing the risen Lord." What does this mean? Was John Wesley's heart-warming experience or Paul's experience on the Damascus road the same as experiencing the risen Lord? Would you say that such an experience may come gradually or must it be a crisis experience? Cite examples to support your view. Methodism is supposed to be experienced religion. Is it? In Wesley's day it was the accepted practice to talk about religious experience; today we rarely speak about it. Why is it that people cannot or do not talk about their religious experience?

Allow time for questions and comments from those who have listened to the discussion.

■ Think about the words, "God With Us." For one minute write on a 3x5 card everything the words symbolize for you. Several persons might share their thoughts with the entire group.

■ Read or sing S/R, 30 as a benediction.

■ Let the leadership team be prepared to make assignments for the next chapter of study and the members of the group be prepared to accept the assignments.

NOTES ON CHAPTER 4

Page 70: Bruce Catton, *This Hallowed Ground* (Doubleday and Company, 1956), pages 256-57. Used by permission.

Understanding the Bible is possible only when we are identified with God's gathered people.

5

□□

TODAY THIS SCRIPTURE HAS
BEEN FULFILLED

One of our purposes in this book is to study selected passages from the Bible so that we may better understand the Bible as a witness to the good news. The study is not just to gain more facts about the Bible. *This study of the Bible is intended primarily to help us realize that God is present in our lives now—at this particular moment—in this specific place.*

This approach to Bible study is not something new. The Bible is a part of our heritage from the past. In connection with our consideration of Exodus 32, we have observed how Old Testament writers understood their past; that the biblical narratives which witnessed to the covenant that God

---

■ *As you arrive at your place of meeting, check the assignment chart for specific preparation to be made before the session begins.*
■ Set goals for your study of this chapter as suggested on page 17.

made with Israel at Mount Sinai were not merely historical accounts of an ancient event. They were used by the Israelites in connection with the great religious celebrations that were observed at such shrines as Bethel and Shechem and later in the temple at Jerusalem. When these narratives were read or recited in the gathered congregation, the people not only remembered what God had done in the past. They also experienced anew his gracious presence and committed themselves to live according to his law.

One of the distinctive marks of the Christian community is the congregation gathered to hear the reading and the proclamation of God's saving word as contained in the Old and New Testaments. The study in which we are now engaged has a history which reaches all the way back to the origins of Hebrew faith in the living God. This history makes us members of the community of God's people— the community which that same God has called into existence in each succeeding generation. Through this study we experience anew God's gracious presence in our lives. As we experience God's presence, we commit ourselves to live according to his purpose. *We have not really grasped the meaning of a biblical text until it becomes the means whereby the living God speaks to us and makes his claim upon our lives.*

■ Use Conversation Three or Four from "Six Conversations" (Resource Packet, item 3). The Leaders' Guide in the packet contains suggestions for its use. See also *S/R,* 38.

■ A woman who recovered from a nervous breakdown is convinced she received strength through constantly holding her mind on the verse, "I can do all things through Christ who strengthens me" (Philippians 4:13). In small groups discuss this and other ways in which God possibly speaks or has spoken to you. What kind of faith do you think God claims from such a person? What kind of behavior should result from such recovery?

Our study of the Bible in the church often falls short of this ideal. That fact is evidence that we can never become complacent about our ability to read and understand the Scripture. Many honest people have sought to deepen their faith through study of the Bible, only to discover that their best efforts lead only to frustration and irrelevance. I am sure that most of us at one time or another have turned to the Bible seeking inspiration, guidance, and strength and have found instead an ancient literature, difficult to read, and seemingly unrelated to our own lives and situations. Most of us, therefore, need all the help we can get when we engage in study of the Bible so that we may find a renewed awareness of the reality of God in our lives and a deepened dedication to his work in the world. (*S/R*, 37.)

One invaluable source of such help that is often ignored or overlooked is the relationship of Jesus himself to the Scriptures of his people. Of course, we must be careful not to read the New Testament accounts of the words and deeds of Jesus as complete reports of his earthly existence. The gospels were not written as objective biographies of Jesus. We know now that the traditions about the life and work of Jesus were collected and preserved by the church *because* they expressed the faith of the church in her risen Lord. The events from the life of Jesus have been recognized as Scripture because in them the good news is proclaimed:

AS HIS CUSTOM WAS

"And he came to Nazareth, where he had been brought up" (Luke 4:16*a*). Evidently Jesus grew up in the village of Nazareth in much the same way as any other first-century Jewish youth. He had been instructed in the practice and content of the Jewish faith, and this faith must have been the most important factor in his environment.

In the synagogue he joined the adult males of the community in reading and studying the Hebrew Scriptures. This study was a regular and systematic exploration of the witness of his people to the presence and power of the living God. Through the study he himself developed a sense of continuity with his people. That is, he felt that he was a part of this community which began at Sinai and continued at Shechem. (See Chapter 2 of this book.) Jesus came to his own self-understanding against this background of the faith of the community. In the community he found the resources for interpreting his own life in his belief that this community was *his* community also as he participated in his hometown congregation gathered for prayer and study in the synagogue on the sabbath day.

Perhaps one of the chief reasons some of us experience frustration and bewilderment as we seek insight into our own lives through Bible study in that we *ignore* what is taken for granted in this narrative. That is: this passage takes for granted that Jesus understood himself to be a part of the history of his people. The background for our understanding the Bible as witness to the good news is participation in the biblical faith; we need to realize that we too are a part of God's gathered people.

The study of the Bible is intensely personal and demands the engagement of our lives at the deepest levels of our concern. It is never a private matter that we can take up or put down at will. If the Bible is a strange book, unrelated to our needs, it may be because we are strangers to the God it proclaims. Perhaps we do not feel that we are a part of the community of faithful persons created by his presence. The church in much of her contemporary life must share responsibility for the fact that many who claim membership in her life have not found opportunities for regular and systematic study of the biblical witness. We cannot go back to the first-century synagogue. Neither can we re-establish the class meeting that John Wesley devised to meet a similar need in eighteenth-century England.

Only when we find the forms suitable for *our* day will many of us experience that nurturing in faith which will enable us to find inspiration, guidance, and strength through Bible study. As long as we continue to receive members into the church without giving them the disciplined participation in the community of faith which Jesus received as he grew up in Nazareth, we will continue to have members who are baffled and bewildered by the biblical witness.

As we look further into this passage, we discover that Jesus' participation in the prayer and study of the synagogue service had helped him become thoroughly at home in the religious heritage of his people. There is nothing to suggest that Jesus had been trained as a professional teacher. The picture presented by Luke is that of a layman who was familiar with the Scriptures. "And he stood up to read; and there was given to him the book of the prophet Isaiah" (Luke 4:16b-17a). The conclusion is that this was not the first time Jesus had assumed the task of reading and interpreting the Scriptures in the synagogue. (S/R, 38.)

Jesus' confidence in the Scriptures is evidence that he had become accustomed to hearing God speak through them.

He opened the book and found the place where it was written,

> "The Spirit of the Lord is upon me,
> because he has anointed me to preach
>   good news to the poor.
> He has sent me to proclaim release to
>   the captives
> and recovering of sight to the blind,
> to set at liberty those who are oppressed,
> to proclaim the acceptable year of the
>   Lord"
>
> (Luke 4:17b-19).

His disciplined participation in the religious life of his people enabled him to draw upon the resources of his heritage to meet the challenge of that moment in the synagogue in Nazareth. The hours of study and prayer which had become a regular part of his existence had prepared him to hear and apply to his own situation the word which God had spoken through the prophet Isaiah.

HOW TO HEAR THE BIBLE SPEAK

Today those who hear the Bible speaking most clearly and powerfully are those who have become thoroughly acquainted with it through years of devoted study. The ability to read and to interpret a passage of Scripture does not come like a flash. It is the result of study and meditation that is carried out on a regular basis over a long period of years. The individual who waits until a moment of crisis to turn to the Bible for guidance, comfort, and strength is often disappointed, because he has failed to develop the insight and sensitivity which are required to hear the word of the Lord.

Each individual must accept responsibility for becoming competent to read and to understand the Bible. Naturally, there are resources available to aid the individual to acquire confidence in hearing what God is saying to him through the biblical witness. But until he himself assumes responsibility for becoming thoroughly at home in the religious heritage of his people, those resources are no help at all.

I wonder how often our programs of adult Christian education fail at this point. For a number of years now we have had excellent material available for those who desire to study the Bible. But for the most part this material has not been used effectively in the church. I suspect that one of the chief reasons is that too many of us have not been willing to make the personal commitment to prayer and study which effective use of such material demands. We have been willing to let someone else talk to us about the Bible and tell us what it says. We have failed, therefore, to develop that familiarity with its contents which would make its resources available for our lives.

■ Use the chart "Biblical Literature" (Resource Packet, item 9).
Example 5 (2 Samuel 1:19-27) is an elegy. Read this passage as
history. What difference does it make to know the type of literature? Let a research team report on the Book of Jonah, using the
chart as background. Ask your minister or church library for commentaries on Jonah or check recent standard encyclopedias (possibly
available in public schools).

■ Study Luke 4:16-30, the passage that is the basis for this chapter.
Use the chart "Study a Portion of the Bible" (Resource Packet, item
2). See the Leaders' Guide, procedure 8.

AS JESUS INTERPRETED THE SCRIPTURES

Jesus did not use the passage he read from Isaiah as the
basis of a lecture on Israel's history. It was a word that he
heard and applied to his own life. Jesus had discerned
certain definite claims upon his life. He was aware
of the hopelessness of the poor, the bondage of the captives,
the affliction of the blind, and the enslavement of the oppressed. (S/R, 39.) He interpreted these claims not simply
as the needs of men but as the revelation of God's will and
purpose for his life. The claim of God which was announced
by the prophet Isaiah was the controlling and motivating
power in Jesus' life. The word which God had spoken
through the prophet was the word that illuminated his own
situation and helped him to understand his life's work. The
point of contact between Jesus' life and the message of the
prophet was the "Spirit of the Lord." Jesus interpreted the
power that he experienced in his own life as nothing less
than the Spirit that Israel had known in the past. The earliest
prophets also were Spirit-endowed men. Both Elijah and
Elisha were made prophets by the gift of the Spirit.

When Jesus said, "Today this scripture has been fulfilled
in your hearing" (Luke 4:21b), he identified the power at
work in his life as the Spirit of the Lord. He saw himself as
the Anointed of the Lord, the Messiah or Christ, who had
been equipped by the Spirit for his saving work.

The response that Jesus made to the word that he heard God speaking to him through the prophet Isaiah is perhaps the most accurate measurement of our ability to read and understand Scripture. Until we hear God speaking to us through our study of a biblical text, we really have no understanding of that passage. The word demands that it be applied to our lives. For example, this particular passage requires that we examine our own lives for signs of God's spirit. But this means that we must acknowledge the Spirit in acts of obedience to God's will for our lives. (S/R, 40.)

■ Write one sentence that expresses the main point of S/R, 40. Compare the attitudes toward those in need expressed in S/R, 39 A-D and 40. See also James 2:14-17. Notice that S/R, 40 says "love and tenderness in your heart . . . excites you to do all that you can." (A Serious Call to the Devout and Holy Life greatly influenced John Wesley.) What would you do, if you really did all you could, about such conditions as described in S/R, 39 A-D? How would your action compare with Matthew 25:31-46?

ALL SPOKE WELL OF HIM

In this narrative Luke reports that after Jesus read and interpreted Isaiah 61:1-2, "all spoke well of him" (Luke 4:22a). The point is that at a certain level the people were quite willing to approve the way Jesus understood and appropriated the religious heritage of Israel. After all, what he had done was quite commendable. He had recognized a bond of solidarity with his people by joining with them in the sabbath service in the synagogue. He had demonstrated that he was a competent and perceptive student of Israel's Scripture by reading and explaining a text from the prophet Isaiah. He had also given an excellent example of personal piety by recognizing the claim of God in the passage and by committing himself to live according to that claim.

So the safe thing to do was to approve what he had done and get back to business as usual in the synagogue as quickly as possible. There was a disturbing emphasis in his interpretation upon serving the poor, the captive, the blind, and the oppressed. But that could effectively be avoided by a few well-chosen words of praise. There was also a compelling note of urgency in his voice which demanded that his hearers commit themselves to the work of the Spirit of the Lord. Such commitment was to be avoided at all cost. The best way to do that was to flatter him and thus avoid the necessity of a decision about what he had said concerning God's work in the world.

The easy acceptance of the ministry of the Word is one of the things we must be on guard against today. (*S/R*, 41.) Most of what is demonstrated in Jesus' use of Scripture in this passage would be applauded in our present-day churches. We think that it is a good thing to maintain a sense of continuity with our religious past. We also approve of a kind of familiarity with the rich resources of our religious heritage. And we are quick to commend the ability to apply the biblical message to our contemporary situation. When someone appears in our churches today who is capable of doing what Jesus did in the synagogue in Nazareth, we speak well of him. *We do this because words of praise are "cheaper" than faithful acts of obedience.*

The true interpretation and application of Scripture demand the acknowledgment of God's claim on our lives and commitment of our resources to his saving work in the world. (*S/R*, 42.) But this kind of personal involvement in the biblical faith is the one thing most of us are determined to avoid. Therefore, we give lip service to Bible study and flatter those who do read and understand the Bible; but we refuse to make the costly decisions God demands.

Those who heard Jesus read and interpret Isaiah 61:1-2 "wondered at the gracious words which proceeded out of his mouth" (Luke 4:22*b*). This indicates that his understanding and use of Scripture was marked by an authority and power which commanded the attention of his hearers.

Today when the Bible is read and interpreted in the congregation by men of faith, it is accompanied by this same authority and power. It commands attention and its message is often received with wonder. But this kind of *interest in* the Word of God must not be confused with the response that God desires when he speaks to men. Wonder is not enough because it does not recognize the authority and power of the interpreter of Scripture as the authority and power of God himself. It is not enough because it requires no decision on the part of the hearer and, therefore, leaves his life exactly as it was before the Word was spoken.

This unfaithful response to the Word of God can be documented over and over again in our contemporary church life. At first glance our crowded churches and devotion to reading and hearing the Bible appear to be a faithful response to God's Word. On closer examination, however, these things turn out to be a concealed rejection of God's claims on our lives. More often than not, we refuse to recognize the power of the ministry of the Word as the power of God. We accept our teachers and preachers as our own, but we refuse to hear them as God's own messengers whose words demand that we submit our lives to the rule of the living God. We speak well of them, wonder at their gracious words, and acknowledge their unusual achievements.

The one thing we are most reluctant to do is recognize that in the faithful interpretation of Scripture God's Holy Spirit is present proclaiming good news to the poor and offering release from captivity, recovery of sight, and liberty from oppression. We are reluctant to make this recognition, because it would expose us to the reality of God in our lives and require us to make a decision for or against him.

ALL WERE FILLED WITH WRATH

The remaining verses of the narrative show that this is a correct interpretation of Luke 4:22. Jesus recognized that the response of the people was a faithless rejection of his ministry. By refusing Jesus' ministry of the Word the people were demanding that Jesus do something more spectacular which would attract their attention. So he said to them, "Doubtless you will quote to me this proverb, 'Physician, heal yourself; what we have heard you did at Capernaum, do here also in your own country'" (Luke 4:23). This was really a stern reproach for those who were so unfaithful to think that there was any miraculous deed which could reveal the presence of God more powerfully than his spoken word. They had refused to hear his witness, and since they were deaf to his word, they would also be blind to any mighty work he might perform. What the Word of God had not been able to accomplish could not be accomplished by the performance of a miracle. Therefore, he said, "Truly, I say to you, no prophet is acceptable in his own country" (Luke 4:24). Again this word of our Lord must be interpreted as a stern reprimand. It was not just a wise saying. But it was a profound summary of Israel's tragic rejection of God's messengers and a penetrating insight into her rebellious resistance to God's ministry in the world.

The point is very clear: the people in the synagogue were guilty of the same stubborn resistance to the Holy Spirit in the ministry of Jesus as were their forefathers in rejecting the ministries of Elijah and Elisha.

We belong to a religious tradition in which the Word of God has been cherished. The question this narrative forces upon us is this: Have we faithfully received the Word and lived according to its power and purpose? The history of the church in general and our own history in particular have often been marked by a continuation of the rejection of God's Word which is so dramatically portrayed in this narrative.

The temptation is to limit our understanding of this rejection to certain obvious and glaring failures of the church to meet the challenge of the social evils of the past and present.

Certainly, we ought to be aware of this dimension of our unfaithfulness, but we must also be aware of a more widespread and serious rejection of God's Word in the church. Even when the Bible is read and interpreted in the church, it is all too frequently looked upon as a purely human enterprise which is in no way related to God's word of grace and judgment.

When we reject the ministry of the Word in the church, we have rejected the Spirit of the Lord. Like those in the Nazareth synagogue, we have identified ourselves with the faithless and rebellious people who rejected Elijah and Elisha and our Lord in Nazareth. Today as in ancient Israel the ministry of the Word of God often finds a more faithful hearing among the outsiders than among the insiders who have been raised in the heritage of the church.

THE WRATH OF THE UNFAITHFUL

One of the surest signs that the Bible is being read and interpreted faithfully is the wrath of the unfaithful. That was the case in Nazareth in the first century, and it is the case in our churches today. The claims that God's Word makes through the Scriptures cannot be avoided. Through the power of the Holy Spirit they are manifest as the Bible is read and studied in the church today.

This is why the honest and open study of the Bible in the church is often accompanied by crisis and controversy. The witness of the Bible confronts the church with the grace and judgment of the living God. Those who give themselves to the interpretation and application of the Scriptures in the church must be prepared for the angry opposition of those who desire to escape God's disturbing and disrupting claims.

Because most of us want to keep our lives running in the customary ruts, we neglect our own study of the Bible and resent and resist those who seek to confront us with its message. If we really heard the biblical witness, our lives would take new directions. We would become bearers of good news to the poor. We would be sent "to proclaim release to the captives and recovering of sight to the blind, to set at liberty those who are oppressed" (Luke 4:18). But because we reject the Word we have no good news and we have no power to enable us to minister. We have risen up against the Spirit of the Lord and have stubbornly driven him out of our lives. But we have not judged God; he has judged us. Passing through the midst of us, he has gone away.

■ Ask four persons in advance to interview a poor person, a blind person, a jail prisoner, and a member of some minority group. Interviewers might begin by asking these questions: Have you ever really been helped by any Christian person or church group? What do you think of the concern of most Christians for people in trouble? Carry on interviews from there. If possible, tape record the interviews and take pictures of those interviewed.

Hear the four reports, and then discuss: How do these reports affect our seriousness about our Bible study as a community of faith? What responses to our study do they suggest?

■ As a closing period of worship, have one person read aloud Script One of the filmslip "Getting Inside the Bible" (Resource Packet, item 1).

■ Let the leadership team be prepared to make assignments and the members of the group to accept the assignments.

"You are all one in union with Christ Jesus." Galatians 3:28.

6

□□

GOD SHOWS NO PARTIALITY

Through the life, death, and resurrection of Jesus the
Spirit of the Lord that rested upon Jesus has fallen upon all
who follow him. This is the testimony of the church from
the first century down to this present moment. In all the
literature of the New Testament the fact that the church is
a Spirit-endowed community is made crystal clear. But the
document that places greatest stress upon this aspect of
church life is the Book of Acts. Although it is called "The
Acts of the Apostles," a more accurate description of its
contents would be "The Acts of the Holy Spirit."

One of the purposes of the Book of Acts was to help the
earliest Christians understand that they had been called and
equipped for ministry by the same Spirit which anointed

■ *As you arrive at your place of meeting, check the assignment chart for
specific preparation to be made before the session begins.*

■ Set goals for your study of this chapter as suggested on page 17.

Jesus "to preach good news to the poor" and which sent him "to proclaim release to the captives and recovering of sight to the blind, to set at liberty those who are oppressed, to proclaim the acceptable year of the Lord" (Luke 4:18-19). It is now generally agreed that the Gospel of Luke and the Book of Acts comprise a two-volume work which Luke wrote to show that the good news of the Spirit-filled life of Jesus was released into human history by the Spirit-endowed life and work of his church. Luke showed this relationship by recording various kinds of events out of the life of the first-century church. But his favorite method was to show how the Holy Spirit gave the church the guidance and strength required to proclaim the good news of Jesus in the face of mounting opposition and resistance.

In Acts 10:1–11:18 Luke reports how the church solved the problem that was created by the inclusion of the Gentiles in her fellowship. Jesus himself had been brought up and had lived as a faithful Jew. We can be fairly certain that his ministry was directed primarily to his people and that his followers were predominantly Jewish. But after his death and resurrection the tremendous creative power released in the church by the gift of the Holy Spirit carried the good news beyond the Jewish community to the Gentiles.

The result was followers of Jesus with two radically different backgrounds: Jewish Christians and Gentile Christians.

The Jewish Christians were first in point of time and occupied the positions of honor and authority in the church. As Jews they had been accustomed to practice careful separation from the Gentiles by keeping the sabbath, observing strict dietary laws, and circumcising their male children. But as Christians they found themselves part of a fellowship where separation from the Gentiles was increasingly difficult.

What should these Jewish Christians do? Should they make the sabbath, the dietary laws, and circumcision conditions which the Gentiles had to fulfill before they could be received into the Christian community? Or should they recognize that in the church they had entered into a new relationship where the old distinctions between Jew and Gentile had been canceled out?

In Acts 10, Luke shows how the Holy Spirit enabled the church to face and solve the Gentile problem.

The situation has changed. Today the church is no longer intimately associated with her Jewish origins. The Gentiles are not a minority seeking admission into the larger fellowship. In the sense that most of her members come from non-Jewish origins, the Gentiles constitute the overwhelming majority of her members. We are the Gentiles and we occupy the positions of honor and authority in the church. So the problem is different. The Holy Spirit is still active in the church including those whose backgrounds socially, culturally, and racially are different from ours.

How shall we meet the challenge of the inclusive fellowship that the Holy Spirit is still creating in the church? Shall we use our positions of honor and authority to demand that all who would enter our fellowship must first conform to our standards and our customs? Or shall we follow the guidance of the Holy Spirit into a fellowship where all the old distinctions have been removed?

So we study Acts 10 not because we are faced with the same problem but because we recognize that only through the guidance and power of the Holy Spirit can we find our way to a solution of the crisis in the church today.

■ Christians are called and equipped to minister by the same Spirit that anointed Jesus. Listen as one member of the group reads aloud Luke 4:18-19. Then the group may observe a period of silence during which time each person will read again the Scripture for this chapter, Acts 10:1–11:18.

■ Let all members of the group participate in an idea inventory. Without discussion, list on newsprint or chalkboard cultural, social, or religious standards or customs that exclude persons from your fellowship (church, class, circle, club). Now discuss in the total group: What steps can we take to make ours an inclusive fellowship in and through which the Holy Spirit is free to work?

A DEVOUT MAN WHO FEARED GOD

It is significant that Luke began this all-important narrative not with a description of the privileges of a Jewish Christian but with the introduction of a God-fearing Gentile. "At Caesarea there was a man named Cornelius, a centurion of what was known as the Italian Cohort, a devout man who feared God with all his household, gave alms liberally to the people, and prayed constantly to God" (Acts 10:1-2). From the point of view of traditional Judaism Cornelius was an outsider. He was excluded from all the normal social relationships of the Jews, because he was considered unclean. Moreover, his presence in Palestine was a hateful sign of the defeat of the Jewish people by the Roman Empire.

The description he gave of Cornelius stressed that even as a Gentile he already possessed those qualities which were admired and sought by every faithful Jew. He and his whole household recognized and worshiped the God of Judaism. He had not become a Jew by submitting to circumcision and by accepting the laws of clean and unclean, but he honored the God of the Jews and sought to conform to the moral standards observed in the Jewish community. His fear or reverence was expressed in acts of charity and in the practice of personal piety. He "gave alms liberally to the people, and prayed constantly to God."

The point which Luke made was that the outsider, contrary to popular Jewish opinion, was not a godless infidel but a God-fearer whose life expressed those virtues which the Jews themselves respected and cultivated.

Luke's sensitive description of Cornelius speaks directly to a crisis in the church today. There is no point in denying that the outsider is a permanent feature in contemporary society. We all have seen the cultural, social, and religious forces that separate the visitor of another country from the mainstream of our life. More pointedly, we have observed the segregation of the Puerto Rican, the Indian, and the Negro that has shut him up in a ghetto and made him an outsider in his own land. And those of us who have traveled abroad have experienced the separation that comes from being regarded as different and being treated as an outsider.

Luke made it clear in this narrative that God's sphere of activity was not restricted to the Jewish community. "About the ninth hour of the day he [Cornelius] saw clearly in a vision an angel of God coming in and saying to him, 'Cornelius' " (Acts 10:3). The distinction between Jew and Gentile was disregarded by God as he revealed himself to this outsider. "And he stared at him in terror, and said, 'What is it Lord?' And he said to him, 'Your prayers and your alms have ascended as a memorial before God' " (Acts 10:4).

The Gentile outsider recognized that he had been visited from on high so he submitted himself to God's command. He in turn was assured by the divine messenger that the piety and charity which he practiced in his life were acceptable to God. Therefore, God himself had already acted to show that the distinctions between Jew and Gentile did not reflect the relationship of God to men. Faithfulness to God demanded that those who had been separated by the laws of men be brought together in an all-inclusive fellowship. So the angel commanded Cornelius to seek to establish a relationship with Peter, a Jew: "Send men to Joppa, and bring one Simon who is called Peter" (Acts 10:5).

These verses confront the church of today with a sobering fact. God's sphere of activity is not limited to those of us who consider ourselves insiders. Even now God is revealing himself behind the Iron and Bamboo Curtains and within the ghetto and Indian reservations. He ignores the barriers that we erect and accepts the worship and service of faithful men without regard for our distinctions of ideology, class, color, and creed. (*S/R,* 43 and 44.) The force that drives the world toward an all-inclusive society is not just the spirit of the age. It is also the power and purpose of God. The most responsive point of contact for the church and the world is where God is breaking down the barriers and preparing the separated people for life together. One practical implication many persons draw from this insight is that the church should use channels of co-operation like the United Nations and the World Council of Churches.

Luke completed his introduction of Cornelius by reporting in the most matter-of-fact way the response of the Gentile to what had been revealed to him. "When the angel who spoke to him had departed, he called two of his servants and a devout soldier from among those that waited on him, and having related everything to them, he sent them to Joppa" (Acts 10:7-8). What a bold assertion he made! The initiative to accomplish God's will for an all-inclusive fellowship did not come from the insiders (Jewish Christians) but from the outsiders (God-fearing Gentiles). (*S/R,* 45.) Without a moment's hesitation or debate, Cornelius explained what had been revealed to him to "two of his servants and a devout soldier" and sent them to make the first breach in the wall which separated Jews and Gentiles.

In most recent times the forces that have attacked the racial barriers in the church have for the most part arisen ouside the church. The initiative has come from the outsiders, from those who have seen the vision and have acted thereon. In our own time we have seen that the pioneering apostles of unity are those whom faithful outsiders have sent to knock at the door of the church. They are God's ministers to us, and they come offering us the opportunity to join with them in achieving a fellowship where all the walls have been broken down.

■ Are God's activity and concern limited to those of us who consider ourselves insiders? Test your attitudes: Mark the blank with an *A* if you agree, a *D* if you disagree, and a *U* if you are uncertain.

_____ A person who does not believe in God should not be allowed to preach his belief to others.

_____ "Love thy neighbor" means that we treat all races alike.

_____ There is no room in the church for persons who believe in communism.

_____ Church people ought to defend the freedom of speech even of those persons whose views are unpopular.

■ Have *S/R* 43, 44, and 50 read aloud while each person follows the reading silently. In groups of five or six discuss: Can we "wash our hands" of persons because of their origins, beliefs, attitudes, or allegiances? Give examples that influence your answer to this question. Are there any limits beyond which the church need not go? If there are, what are they? How is the church's ministry limited by the tendency to write off the outsider as godless? Give some examples of deficiencies in your own church's (and your own group's) ministry caused by this attitude toward the outsider.

GOD HAS SHOWN ME

Having introduced Cornelius, Luke reports how the church was prepared to meet the crisis triggered by Cornelius' revelation. But before we consider this stage of the event, let us recall once more our purpose for studying this passage. Our concern is not merely to consider an interesting development in the history of the church; but it is also to become aware of and responsive to the power and guidance of the Holy Spirit. This means that as we study to determine what Luke wrote about Cornelius and Peter we must also listen faithfully for the word that God is speaking through this narrative to us. We recognize that now, as then, God is speaking to his church to prepare her to do his work in the world.

The first point that Luke made was that Peter was open to God's guidance. "The next day, as they were on their journey and coming near the city, Peter went up on the housetop to pray, about the sixth hour" (Acts 10:9). Here prayer was not something that Peter said to God but the attitude of dependence and trust that characterized his life.

93

In the act of prayer, Peter as a representative of the church displayed the fact that the church was responsive to the power and presence of God and ready to obey his commands.

Perhaps there is no point in contemporary church life where the barrenness of our religious life is so apparent as in our failure to pray. We often wonder why our lives are not filled by the power of God and shaped by his purpose. The reason is not that we have failed to say things to God but simply that we have failed to submit our lives to him in trust and dependence. Most of us desire to become effective instruments in performing God's work in the world. But there is no chance that our desire will be realized unless we open our lives in prayer so that God may speak and we may hear.

■ Continue in small groups. Read silently Matthew 5:43-48; 6:5-14; 21:22; Luke 11:1-13; and James 5:13-16.
Think silently: When or in what circumstances do I pray? What does this say about my prayer life? What new understandings of the purpose and power of prayer come from the Scripture just read? You may wish to share your insights with the group.
Discuss: Does your experience with prayer support the idea that failure to pray is also failure to trust God for strength and guidance, or are you aware of other causes for lack of power in prayer?
Share: Has anyone in the group ever opened his life to God in prayer and experienced positive guidance? healing? change in attitude toward others? help in political, occupational, social decisions? How does that experience compare with Peter's (Acts 10:9-35)?

The immediate result of Peter's openness to God's guidance was an experience of revelation. (*S/R,* 46.) "He fell into a trance and saw the heaven opened, and something descending, like a great sheet, let down by four corners upon the earth" (Acts 10:10*b*-11). The tendency to become preoccupied with the details of *how* this occurred must not be allowed to distract our attention from Luke's proclamation *that* it happened. The content of the revelation emphasized

94

that this was an otherworldly experience but one which focused upon this world and the crisis in the earthly history of the church.

> "In it were all kinds of animals and reptiles and birds of the air. And there came a voice to him, 'Rise, Peter; kill and eat.' But Peter said, 'No Lord; for I have never eaten anything that is common or unclean.' And the voice came to him again a second time, 'What God has cleansed, you must not call common'" (Acts 10:12-15). (S/R, 47.)

As we have already mentioned, one of the barriers to the admission of the Gentiles into full fellowship in the church was the observance of strict dietary laws by the Jewish Christians. These verses meet the problem head on. In a vision Peter saw all kinds of food he had been taught not to eat because they were ritually unclean. The voice ordered him to eat. So the purpose of the revelation was to establish that God had declared that the Jewish laws of clean and unclean did not apply to the Christian community. In order to remove the resistance of Peter and to make absolutely clear the binding force of the event, "this happened three times, and the thing was taken up at once to heaven."

A conclusion that we are forced to draw on the basis of this narrative is that God gives visions to the faithful not for their private meditation but in order to illuminate those problems that threaten to destroy human life.

The precise meaning of what Peter experienced on the housetop in prayer was in response to the claim that the world made upon him. (S/R, 48.) "While Peter was inwardly perplexed as to what the vision which he had seen might mean, behold, the men that were sent by Cornelius, having made inquiry for Simon's house, stood before the gate and called out to ask whether Simon who was called Peter was lodging there" (Acts 10:17-18). The work of the Holy Spirit in this situation was to make Peter sensitive and obedient to the request that the men brought. "While Peter was pondering the vision, the Spirit said to him, 'Behold, three men are looking for you. Rise and go down, and accompany them without hesitation; for I have sent them' " (Acts 10:19-20). The claim which was expressed in the presence of the three messengers from an outsider was not an interruption to be resisted but a command of God to be obeyed.

Peter did more than ponder the vision; he also acted upon the understanding that it brought to him. As Peter went down to these Gentile messengers, he left centuries of Jewish custom behind and entered into a new community that God had created in Jesus Christ.

GOD'S MESSENGERS TO US

Today those who discern the meaning of God's revelation are those who respond to the needs of the world. (S/R, 49.) The men who cry out in distress bring to the church her orders from God. They are messengers sent from God to us so that instead of being left to ponder the meaning of what we have seen we confidently may understand and obey God's will for our lives. The fact that the church is sometimes sensitive and obedient to the claims which God makes through human need is evidence that the Holy Spirit is still active within her life. The appropriate response of the church is to make herself available to those who knock at her door. The church can only do this by understanding that God is already available to men in need and that she cannot be with God unless she joins him in ministering to the needs of men. (S/R, 50.) The "housetop" is the place where the church at prayer experiences revelation; but the place where she understands the meaning of revelation is in the street. There the church is brought face to face with the fact that God has placed no limits upon his love, and therefore, the church cannot place limits upon her love without being unfaithful.

The key to interpreting the series of events that ended in the meeting between Cornelius and Peter was not some divine quality in the life of Peter (Acts 10:25-26.) Instead, it was the power and presence of the living God before whom there was no distinction between Cornelius and Peter, between Gentile and Jew. The most important thing for both Peter and Cornelius to know about each other was simply that they were men. Peter had learned that there was nothing in his life which made him superior and likewise that there was nothing in Cornelius' life which made him inferior. Before God they stood on the same ground as equals.

This provided the opportunity for Peter to share his understanding of what he had experienced. He said to the kindred and close friends who had gathered with Cornelius' household, "You yourselves know how unlawful it is for a Jew to associate with or to visit any one of another nation; but God has shown me that I should not call any man common or unclean. So when I was sent for, I came without objection" (Acts 10:28-29a). Cornelius had been sprung free from his pagan background. Peter also had been released from the bondage of Jewish legalism that separated him from Gentiles. The power that had brought this about was not a historical accident or a fortunate combination of political and cultural forces. The power came from the disclosure of God's presence and purpose in the lives of men.

The only justification Peter offered for his association with Gentiles, his receiving them in his own home and his visiting them in theirs, was that he had acted according to what God had shown him. The messengers from Cornelius brought God's order for his life. Others might object to what he had done. But that did not matter, because God had shown him what he had to do and thus made it impossible for any real objections to be raised. Peter had come to Cornelius according to God's will; he awaited further instructions.

The need of men requires that the church break every

97

custom or prejudice which separates her from intimate association with those in need. This will certainly not be done without arousing the opposition of those who are ignorant of God's will or who are unfaithful and disobedient. The recent efforts of churchmen to break the color barrier in the church—and to achieve a society where *all* forms of segregation, such as social class, status, religion, national origin, and the like have been removed—have been accompanied by objection from within and without the church. These objections must be answered, and they must be answered on the right grounds. The only justification the church has or needs for associating with Puerto Ricans, Indians, Negroes, and the like and identifying with their struggle is what God has shown her about the equality of all men in his presence. There is no such thing as a superior or inferior race. Before God, we are all persons.

This means that no man may lord it over another or use another for his own advantage. The force that has brought men of all nations and races into intimate social relationships is not the natural flow of events but the expression of God's power and purpose in human history. God has sent for the church to join him in breaking down the walls. The church must go without objection or deny her nature and calling.

■ The Bible contains numerous examples of times when God chose to make himself vivid (reveal himself) to persons. Read Exodus 3:1-4; 1 Samuel 3:1-10; Jeremiah 1:4-10; and Acts 8:26-39.

As you discuss these, remember that our concern with these stories is not to determine *how* the revelation occurred but to understand that human life is not cut off from divine influence. See also *S/R*, 46.

What do all of the examples have in common? What conditions or circumstances must exist before God can reveal himself? At those times when God's presence to you has been vivid or intense, have you thought of it as revelation? Why or why not? What change did those experiences bring about in your feelings? your thinking? your attitudes? your behavior? Does God use non-Christians as channels for revelation? Cite examples if you can.

THE WORD WHICH HE SENT

But what was God's purpose in bringing Cornelius and Peter together? Why had Cornelius sent for Peter and why had he been kind enough to come? The answer as Luke understood it has been preserved for us in the last half of verse 33: "Now therefore we are all here present in the sight of God, to hear all that you have been commanded by the Lord." These words from Cornelius suggest that in all that had happened God had been at work preparing the way for the gospel to be preached to the Gentiles. The risen Lord had told his disciples in Jerusalem "that repentance and forgiveness of sins should be preached in his name to all nations" (Luke 24:47). Now Peter was learning what this saying meant for him and his ministry.

What is God's purpose for us as he continues to work in the world to break down the walls that separate us from each other? Through modern means of communication and transportation, the church as never before plainly sees the needs of men. Why are we in this situation? Because God wants us here and has put us here to proclaim to the nations what we have received from the risen Lord.

This may sound like old stuff to some of us. As a matter of theory it is. The church has been talking about it for twenty centuries. But as a program of responsible and creative *action,* the claim of the world on us and on the church is the most powerful new force any of us will ever experience. *The way to renewal in the church does not lead through retreats from the world but through courageous advances into those areas of world crisis where God wants us to be present and available.* And in order to be available we must listen to what God is even now saying to us through the needs of the world.

The most important thing that Peter could do for Cornelius was to confess his Easter faith. God had singled Peter out to be a witness of the Resurrection; not to give him a special privilege but to use him to transmit the power of the risen Lord to every following age. So Peter declared that God made the risen Lord manifest: "not to all the people but to us who were chosen by God as witnesses, who ate and drank with him after he rose from the dead" (Acts 10:41). The power of the risen Lord was revealed in all the events that brought Peter and Cornelius together.

The fact that you and I now share in the faith of the church is evidence that Peter's interpretation of his meeting with Cornelius was correct. Through the witness of Peter and the first believers, the gospel has been transmitted to us Gentiles. That witness has been preserved from age to age in the documents of the New Testament. As we read and study them today, we experience our acceptance before God and we hear the word which he sent to Israel. The Spirit-filled life of Jesus comes to us. His ministry is a present reality, because the witness of the church offers him to us not as a past event but as the *risen* Lord. The gospel we hear inspires our faith, and we receive forgiveness of our sins.

But this Scripture calls us to identify ourselves not only with those who *receive* the gospel but also with those who are commissioned to *proclaim* it. In our dependence upon the witness of the church, we are Cornelius; in our experience of the risen Lord, we are Peter. We have eaten and drunk with our Lord at his table in the Lord's Supper. He has commanded us to preach to the people. Therefore, in obedience we must make our lives channels through whom "the good news of peace" is carried "to the end of the earth" (read Acts 1:6-11).

In fulfilling this mission our most important resource is that which has been transmitted to us. The gospel that we are to proclaim is the word that God sent to Israel, "the word which was proclaimed throughout all Judea, beginning from Galilee after the baptism which John preached." When the world knocks at our door, we do not have to formulate a new gos-

100

pel. We simply have to follow the risen Lord into a new place and there witness faithfully to what we have received. (S/R, 51.) Through our witness "every one who believes in him receives forgiveness of sins through his name." In the life, death, and resurrection of Jesus God has given himself for all men. When the church is faithful in preaching this "good news of peace by Jesus Christ (he is Lord of all)," all who hear and believe are filled with God's power and made aware of his presence.

■ Now read S/R, 35 and 36. Did you encounter any new ideas about the Resurrection? Talk about them. How can we experience resurrection through personal relationships, through acceptance and love, through good will?

■ You have reached mid-point in this unit of study. Take time now to evaluate your group life and study. Use the chart "The Nineteenth Hole" (Resource Packet, item 8). Explicit directions can be found in the Leaders' Guide in the packet.

■ Close the session with prayer.

■ Let the leadership team be prepared to give assignments for the next chapter of study and the members of the group be prepared to accept assignments.

■ At this point it is time to place your order for the third unit of Foundation Studies in Christian Faith, We Have This Heritage: The Church as Witness to the Good News.

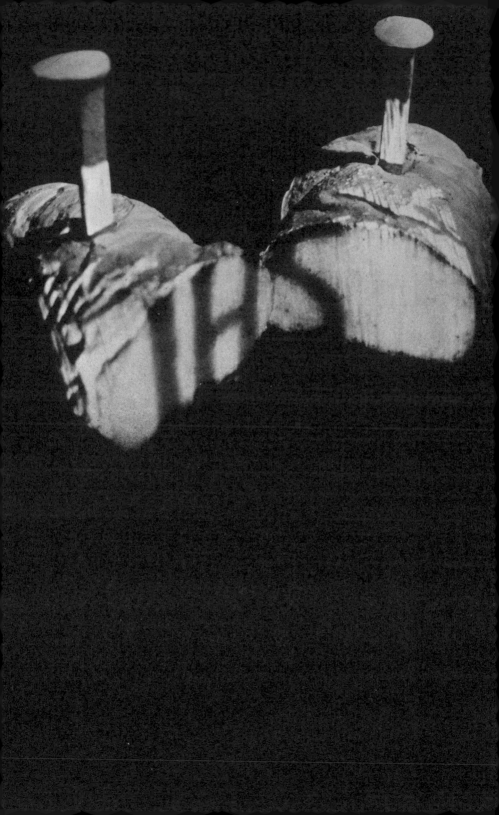

Covenant – Promise of God to Man –
includes an obligation – ↗

7

□□□

THIS IS MY BLOOD OF THE COVENANT

In the narrative that described how Cornelius and Peter were brought together in ancient Caesarea, we saw God at work in human history, breaking down the barriers that separate men from each other. One of the conclusions we drew from our study of Acts 10 is that God desires all men to dwell together in unity and that he has acted decisively in the life, death, and resurrection of Jesus to achieve this purpose.

But why then does our history contain so much evidence that we are still separated from each other? How can we affirm that God acts powerfully in human history when on every hand we are faced with the fact that men resist his will and frustrate his purposes? These questions are forced upon

■ *As you arrive at your place of meeting, check the assignment chart for specific preparation to be made before the session begins.*

■ Set goals for your study of this chapter as suggested on page 17.

us not by idle speculation but by the experience of hostility and separation in our own lives.

As we examine our own lives in the light of what Luke wrote about Cornelius and Peter, we see that one of the chief reasons God's work is not done in the world is our unfaithfulness. (S/R, 52.) Perhaps this understanding of our situation is a shock to you. It always comes as a shock to me! But study of the Bible always confronts us with the shocking truth about ourselves. Mark 14:12-25 is a mirror in which we behold our own lives. The reason we are not reconciled to our neighbors and are not ministers of reconciliation is that we have been unfaithful to God.

Our experience then is not an indictment of God. God has not failed. From the earliest beginnings of Israelite history down to this present moment in the life of the church, the witness of his people is that he has acted faithfully. The tragedy of the Old Testament is not that God broke the agreement which he made with Israel at Mount Sinai but that, in spite of all that God gave his people in that agreement, they were unfaithful to him. Here we are brought face to face with one of the fundamentals of biblical faith. The witness of the biblical narratives is not to the righteousness of men but to the steadfast love of God.

The good news that comes to us in the Bible is the witness of forgiven sinners. This good news addresses us as sinners, and it is directed toward bringing us to that trust and confidence in God which will enable us to receive its consequence: the forgiveness of our sins. The life, death, and resurrection of Jesus are the events through which the first Christian witnesses experienced the forgiveness of their sins. (S/R, 53.)

■ Discuss: Is it possible that God respects our personal dignity enough that he does not destroy the possibility of our keeping secrets from him? How would such respect for privacy lead to our need for confession?

104

THEY PREPARED THE PASSOVER

This narrative of the Last Supper was written by Mark many years after the resurrection of Jesus. He wrote it not primarily to report a historical event but to confess his faith in the risen Lord. The narrative has been preserved in the church because it has proved to be an effective means of creating in the lives of those who read it the faith which moved Mark to write it.

Our first task then is to ask ourselves what Mark proclaimed about the risen Lord in this passage. In answering this question we will come not only to a clearer understanding of the words of the text but also to a more sensitive awareness of the claims of the risen Lord on our lives.

Mark began his report of this event from the last days of Jesus' earthly ministry by setting it in the context of the Jewish Feast of Passover. "And on the first day of Unleavened Bread, when they sacrificed the passover lamb, his disciples said to him, 'Where will you have us go and prepare for you to eat the passover?'" (Mark 14:12). In the framework of the Feast of Passover, the narrative of the Last Supper relates the life, death, and resurrection of Jesus to the central redemptive act of the Old Testament: the deliverance of the Hebrews from Egyptian bondage. Mark has told us in this opening verse that the same God who acted in the Exodus from Egypt had also acted in Jesus of Nazareth to deliver his people from bondage.

The Feast of Passover was a ritualistic re-enactment of the event in which the death angel passed over the homes of the Hebrews in Egypt and killed the first-born of the Egyptians to force them to let God's people go free. The feast was more than a memory of the past. It was a means of grace whereby the faithful of each generation experienced the liberating and redeeming power of God.

■ Display "A Timeline of the Biblical Story" (Resource Packet, item 5). See the Leaders' Guide in the packet for interpretation. As one possibility, make three columns on newsprint or chalkboard: (1) persons, (2) ideas, (3) events. Ask the group to recall out of Israel's past (in Old Testament and New Testament) as many of these as they can. (Hebrews 12 might be read as a "pump primer.") List the items in the proper columns. Relate various points to the timeline, if possible. Then discuss: How does God reveal himself to us through this heritage?

For Mark, the central redemptive event was no longer the Exodus. He had experienced a power greater than that revealed at the deliverance from Egypt. So he undertook in this narrative to present Jesus as the Lord of the feast who was in complete charge of all that took place. The disciples asked Jesus: "Where will you have us go and prepare for you to eat the passover?" The answer to his disciples' question was a prediction of what they would find when they entered Jerusalem: "And he sent two of his disciples, and said to them, 'Go into the city, and a man carrying a jar of water will meet you; follow him'" (Mark 14:13). This verse reflects a recollection of how Jesus and his followers found a place to eat the Passover during his earthly ministry. But *as Mark used it here,* writing as he was more than thirty years after the event, he was proclaiming that the *risen Lord exercised absolute authority among his followers* and issued the commandments they were to obey.

In the last verse of this paragraph Mark described the faithful response which the power and presence of the risen Lord created in the lives of his followers. "The disciples set out and went to the city, and found it as he had told them; and they prepared the passover" (Mark 14:16). There was command and promise in the experience of the risen Lord. He demanded obedience: his followers had to set out according to his orders. But he kept his word: those who obeyed found a place to be with him.

■ Study the Scripture passage to which this chapter is related (Mark 14:12-25). Use the chart "Study a Portion of the Bible" (Resource Packet, item 2, procedure 6). Give attention to this question:

How did Mark's faith in the risen Lord influence his writing of the narrative concerning the Passover meal and the whole gospel?

This narrative confronts us with the assertion that the most powerful force operating in our world to save us from the bondage of sin and death is the risen Lord. We are led to see that the deepest meaning of God's work in human life is made clear by the ministry of the risen Lord. By its very nature the Bible deals primarily with what *has been* done. Even the hope for the future is based upon what has been accomplished by God in the lives of men.

How do we get from the past into our present situation? The answer is that the risen Lord is the present expression of God's power in our lives. Through him we are taught to understand the past in such a way that it becomes effective in our lives today. After all, the reason we study the Bible is to understand how God has been with his people in the past so that we may recognize his presence with us now.

Guidance and direction for the life of the church are available if the modern disciples will only inquire of the risen Lord: "Where will you have us go and prepare for you to be with us in our need?" Through this narrative the risen Lord challenges us to commit our lives to him who is in absolute control of every situation. His is a commanding presence. He orders us to go. His is a knowing presence. There should be no place where we cannot find room for him to be with us. We begin our study of a passage such as this perplexed by the problems it raises for our understanding. But the more we penetrate into its meaning for our lives, the more we realize that it confronts us with a decision concerning the center of our loyalty.

LOYALTY AND OBEDIENCE

These verses help us to see that the question of our faithfulness is basically a matter of our obedience. (*S/R*, 54.) If the Teacher is the center of our loyalty, we will live so that his presence will be demonstrated in our actions. We will go into the strange rooms of our cities and claim them as guest rooms of our Lord where he will be present to reveal himself. Faithfulness is not just a matter of what we confess with our lips. It is also what we do with our lives. The risen Lord is the sovereign ruler of every aspect of human life. If we are not conscious that we are going into the whole sweep of human experience to claim it for our Lord, then we have every reason to believe that we are unfaithful to him.

■ Let a committee, previously recruited, be prepared to present a court trial of a Christian who is accused of being disobedient and unfaithful to the authority of Christ. Base the evidence for both sides on *S/R,* 54 and 55, plus the above paragraphs. A hint: look for forms of obedience called for by these readings. Let the entire group serve as the jury. If the accused is found guilty, let the sentence be the result of discussion and let it be taken as a personal sentence by each member who will accept it.

One of the results of reading Mark's witness (he was very sensitive to the presence of the risen Lord in his life) is the haunting awareness that we are often insensitive to our Lord's presence in our lives. Why does this happen to us? Certainly, it is not because the risen Lord is absent. The reason is simply that in refusing to obey him we cut ourselves off from him.

I can recall an experience of my childhood similar to one many of you have had. After a day of careless and thoughtless neglect of the chores which had been assigned to me by my parents, I was suddenly faced with their displeasure. I was not punished in any physical way but I knew that my conduct was not acceptable. The standards of our home had been broken. That night as I was lying in my bed I felt strangely cut off and separated from those who loved and cared for me. My parents had not left our home but my disobedience had created a wall that effectively shut them out of my life. In order to experience their presence in a satisfactory way, I

108

had to tell them I was sorry and start acting according to their standards. (*S/R,* 56.)

■ Invite a juvenile judge, youth parole officer, school guidance counselor, or other youth worker to be interviewed by the group on the point of view expressed in *S/R,* 56 and the preceding paragraph. Some questions to ask the guest should be written out beforehand. One question might deal with the attitude toward obedience to authority on which the guest and his institution operate.

ONE OF YOU WILL BETRAY ME

The word that the Lord spoke was not about himself but about men. His presence revealed the depth of the hostility and rebellion that God always experienced among men, even among those whom he had chosen. "Jesus said, 'Truly, I say to you, one of you will betray me, one who is eating with me'" (Mark 14:18*b*). Mark was not just recording what Judas had done. He was also stating that betrayal was a permanent part of the life of the church. (We must remember that when Mark wrote his gospel the church had already been in existence for more than thirty years.)

"They began to be sorrowful, and to say to him one after another, 'Is it I?'" (Mark 14:19). The experience of the Resurrection enabled unfaithful men to face their failure and to be sorry. Sorry for what? Sorry for joining other unfaithful men in the crucifixion of their Lord. But Mark was not just telling about what had happened in the past. He was also expressing what the church had discovered about her relationship to the risen Lord. The fact that he had been raised from the dead had not removed the possibility of betrayal from the lives of those in the church to whom he had appeared.

ATTACK FROM WITHIN

The fundamental attack upon the community of faith arose not without but within. The answer of Jesus to the questioning disciples drove this point home. "He said to them, 'It is one of the twelve, one who is dipping bread in the same dish with me' " (Mark 14:20). The risen Lord was exposed to betrayal by those whom he had gathered round him through the power of his gracious presence. The church was opposed by powerful external foes, but the enemy that endangered her very life was unfaithfulness in her own household. (S/R, 57.)

■ Display the picture "Christ and Missile" (Resource Packet, item 6). Divide into small groups and read S/R, 57 and Acts 5:1-10. After the silent reading of the assigned materials, carry out the procedure suggested in the Leaders' Guide in the packet.

Judas had attempted to turn Jesus away from the sovereignty of service. In doing so Judas had destroyed himself. Mark knew that the church had not settled the matter with the death of Judas. It had to be settled over and over again in concrete decisions for the life of the risen Lord, the life of humble service. It was a matter of life or death, so he wrote: "Woe to that man by whom the Son of man is betrayed! It would have been better for that man if he had not been born" (Mark 14:21b).

Once more as we reflect upon the implications of this passage for our own self-understanding, we are called to recognize the presence of the risen Lord with us. He is here not because of some special insight that we possess but because it is his nature to give himself for us. Our faith is built upon the fact that he shows himself in the common experiences of ordinary men who are looking and listening for him. (S/R, 58.)

The community of faith, the church, must not be confused with some kind of sacred society of the self-righteous. The church harbors no illusions about her life, because she understands herself in relationship to her Lord. In light of the Lord's faithfulness, obedience, and power, the church understands her own unfaithfulness, disobedience, and weakness.

110

The presence of the risen Lord in the church is judgment of the church. This is one of the ways God puts us to the test. If we really hear Mark proclaiming the Word of God to us, then we must surely be aware of our betrayal of our Lord. Also, if we do not begin to be sorrowful and to say to him one after another, "Is it I?", then it is a sign that we have no sense of his presence.

This narrative also speaks to the current tendency to find the threat to the life of the church in some conspiracy outside the church. Of course, the church must never come to terms with atheistic communism. But the anticommunist crusades that have sprung up in the church in recent years tend to divert attention from the expressions of unfaithfulness within the church herself. The betrayal of the risen Lord that threatens to destroy the life of the church comes from within, not from without, from those of us who dip bread in the same dish with him.

What form does this betrayal take? The same old form of Judas: the denial that God's true power in the world is the life of humble service. Jesus, the Son of man, gave himself in service to the needs of men and refused to defend himself when they turned against him. He has been raised from the dead, but his risen power is not different from the power he demonstrated in his earthly ministry. The two are the same. Now, as the risen Lord, he shows his sovereign authority in offering himself through the preaching of the church and in waiting for men to decide for or against him. (S/R, 59.)

■ Individually, read S/R, 58 and 59. Then sketch out, or write out, or tell another person: If you were going to paint a picture of Jesus' crucifixion, what features would you have in it? What feelings would you try to express? What forms and colors would you use? What would the picture mean to you? Why not try it?

Although the risen Lord gives himself to those who betray him, betrayal may not be taken lightly. "Woe to that man

by whom the Son of man is betrayed!" This word of judgment reminds us that if we refuse to accept the *servant* life
of our Lord and refuse to join him in a life of humble service
we set ourselves against the sovereign power of God himself.
God will not force us to conform to his will for our lives. He
allows us to make our choices, and he has established an order
where our choices determine our destiny.

Those choices of ours which reject his kingdom of humble
service shut us off from his presence and power and consign
us to the weakness and ruin of life without God. The risen
Lord reveals to us that God is present in our world as a
servant, and he calls us to realize our own true life by joining
him in ministering to the needs of men. (*S/R*, 60.) If we
refuse his call to minister to others by accepting the way of
privilege and violence, it would have been better for us if
we had not been born.

■ Quickly read *S/R*, 60. One form of ministry is to begin where
we are—to *be* servants of one another in a group like yours. Use
"The Nineteenth Hole" (Resource Packet, item 8) —a form of
evaluation for your group's work together. The Leaders' Guide
in the packet contains suggestions for its use.
How can the members of your group express enough concern for
members outside the group to lead those outside to want to join
you?

THIS IS MY BODY. . . . THIS IS MY BLOOD

The picture Mark presented was the traditional celebration of the Feast of Passover in a Jewish home. The father
presided at the table and led the family in the symbolic re-
enactment of the deliverance from Egypt. In the church,
according to Mark's understanding, the risen Lord led the
congregation through the symbols of the Lord's Supper into
an ever-new experience of God's redeeming power in their
lives. Because the Lord had been raised from the dead, the
giving of himself on the cross was not an isolated event in the
past. It was not just a historical occurrence. It was the mark

of his continued presence in the world. He was the host who offered himself in every strengthening experience of life.

"And he took a cup, and when he had given thanks he gave it to them, and they all drank of it" (Mark 14:23). Mark's purpose was to move beyond a simple event of the past to proclaim a recurring experience in the life of the church. The risen Lord ministered to the needs of men not on the basis of merit in their lives but on the basis of his own abiding concern for them. *All* without distinction were included in what he offered and *all* without distinction shared in his ministry. "They all drank of it," even Judas.

Just as the meaning of the bread was interpreted by the risen Lord so the meaning of the cup was made plain by him. "And he said to them, 'This is my blood of the covenant, which is poured out for many'" (Mark 14:24). The cup that he offered was his servant life. That life of suffering and self-giving was the basis of the covenant or agreement which God made with men. It was no cheap agreement but one which had been revealed in the world in the blood of a faithful man. That revelation was still going on in the ministry of the risen Lord as he poured out his sovereign power in humble service.

THE EVERLASTING COVENANT

The agreement that God had made with men was not a temporary arrangement. As an expression of the nature and purpose of God, it was an everlasting agreement. Men could resist it, deny it, betray it; but they could not destroy it. They could only destroy themselves. In order to keep them from destruction, God had acted in the life, death, and resurrection of Jesus and he continued to act in the risen Lord.

These verses are a living part of our worship together in the church. The Last Supper has become the Lord's Supper. It is celebrated regularly in the Christian church as a sign of the abiding presence of the risen Lord. (*S/R*, 61). Our participation in this ritual is a constant reminder that the suffering and death of Jesus is not something which happened long ago; it is the repeated experience of the risen Lord. Through his offering of himself, our resistance to him is overcome. He offers us the bread of our life not in any magical or mysterious sense but in the daily support and provision which God gives all his children. When we eat the communion bread, we are confessing that the whole world is sustained and ruled by the self-giving love of God.

Our participation in the Lord's Supper does more than just reflect the individual condition of our souls. It is also a public act in which we confess that God is offered and received by *all* the world regardless of the response of men. The ministry of the risen Lord is not limited by the faithfulness of men. If that were the case, we would find ourselves without God and without hope in the world. God is faithful; he does not deny himself.

When we gather at the Lord's table, we celebrate the agreement that God has made with us. As we take the bread and drink from the cup, we declare that the agreement is everlasting. Through it we find the guidance and strength we need. By accepting what is offered to us, we confess that our lives are maintained not by ourselves but by the grace—the unmerited love—of God. We also proclaim that the covenant we enjoy has been given to us at great cost. What we receive is made possible by a body which is broken and blood which is poured out in faithful service. God does not easily overlook our betrayal of our Lord nor does he accept what *we* have made of our lives. He accepts us as we are in order that he might make us obedient instruments of his purpose.

So in the presence of the broken body and poured out blood of our Lord we become aware of the depth of our sins, and we experience what great price has been paid to forgive our sins.

114

The good news of God's forgiving love which we experience through the presence of the risen Lord in the life of the church is not limited to the church. The Lord's Supper is the Lord's, not ours. The relationship which he establishes with us by the power of his self-giving love is intended "for many." Therefore, the celebration of the Lord's Supper in the church must not be an occasion for withdrawal from the world. Instead, it must be celebrated so that the whole world is kept in view and so that the love of God for the world is made manifest. If we try to restrict the inclusiveness of God's gift of himself, we demonstrate that we have rebelled against him and have not really received his broken body and poured out blood.

God's gift of himself calls forth concrete and specific acts of obedience. The life of love and service *does* find expression in the deeds of ordinary men and women. Our Lord is present not only as the one whom we resist and betray but also as the one whom we receive and serve. The *old* way may persist in our lives, but it has been overcome. The *new* is here. The kingdom has come in the faithful response of our fellowship.

■ Pray together aloud the hymn "Were You There When They Crucified My Lord?" (*S/R*, 81).
■ Let the leadership team be prepared to give assignments for the next chapter of study and the members of the group be prepared to accept assignments.

*The truth about the human situation
is not ugliness, meanness, and hopelessness.*

8

□□□□□□□□□□□□□□□□□□□□□□□□□□□□□□□□□□□□□□□

HAVE THIS MIND AMONG YOURSELVES

We are proud of our ability to see things as they really are. As modern men we have no patience with fairy tales and the world of make-believe. The art and literature that appeal to us most powerfully present life as it actually is, not as it might have been or as it ought to be. We are suspicious of stories that always have a happy ending. We tend to reject the possibility that men and women "live happily ever after." We are also quick to tune out the poet or artist or dramatist who always preaches a sermon to lift the level of our conduct. We have generally dismissed all forms of sentimentalism and romanticism and have placed our highest value upon a realistic approach to life.

■ *As you arrive at your place of meeting, check the assignment chart for specific preparation to be made before the session begins.*
■ Set goals for your study of this chapter as suggested on page 17.

This is one of those aspects of contemporary life where the witness of the Bible speaks most pointedly to our condition. If we want realism, the Bible will not disappoint us. For example, the narratives in the Book of Samuel that describe how David established himself as king and defended his rule against all rivals are as vivid and down to earth as anything in modern literature. King David is presented as a real human being, not as an ideal figure. Political intrigue and violent emotions are set forth in their fierce conflict.

One is also impressed by the realism that characterizes the descriptions of the disciples and the early church in the New Testament. The only way one can maintain the notion that the first Christians were perfect examples of faith and virtue is by ignoring the literature which was produced about them. The documents of the New Testament reveal men and women struggling with the fundamental issues of life, and they make no attempt to portray them except as frail and fallible human beings.

The realism of the biblical view of men, however, cannot be grasped if we confine our understanding of it to descriptions of men's relationships to each other and their physical environment. From the biblical point of view, any attempt to understand the life of man as nothing more than his interaction with other human beings and his struggle to secure the necessities of life is false and unrealistic. Here the biblical writers are very emphatic: man's true life is his life before God and every interpretation which fails to take this into account is a distortion of the human situation. (S/R, 62.)

Of course, for the person who has rejected the biblical faith, this view of man is a fairy tale that must be discarded as an outworn superstition. There is no way to prove by logical argument and objective evidence that the biblical view of man is true. We have accepted it because the life and history of the church have helped us to become aware of

118

God's power and presence in our lives. The reality of God with us has made it possible for us to believe. Our task is not to *defend* the truth but to commit ourselves to it and live so that it will be manifested in what we say and do.

■ Is your church helping persons become aware of the power and presence of God? Have a research team, assigned in advance, present in written form (on newsprint or individual mimeographed sheets) the program of activities of your church over the past year. How did each activity contribute to persons' awareness of God's power and presence? How many of the activities were geared to serve beyond the church? How would you describe the concerns of your church in light of its program of activities? What changes would you suggest? What individual responsibility are you willing to accept for bringing about change? What does S/R, 1 say to your situation?

DO NOTHING FROM SELFISHNESS

Paul probably wrote his letter to the Philippians near the end of his life while in prison at Rome. He had founded the Philippian church during his second missionary journey and had maintained an intimate relationship with the congregation from that time on. During his Roman imprisonment messengers passed back and forth fairly frequently. The letter to Philippi was sent by such a messenger to give the Philippians the benefit of the apostle's advice concerning certain problems which had arisen in the church.

One of the most serious problems was the breakdown of Christian unity. The passage that we are considering in this chapter, Philippians 2:1-11, deals with this particular problem.

Paul did not give in to the temptation to paint a vivid picture of the divisions that had broken out in the church. They were there, and he did not ignore them. But he knew something about the Philippian church that was more fundamental than the frailty and weakness of men. The church had been founded upon what God had done in Christ.

The force of the apostle's thought comes through to us when we translate verse one as follows: "Because there is encouragement in Christ, incentive of love, participation in the Spirit, affection and sympathy. . . ." Paul knew the reality of the life which the church had received in Christ. He knew that it was more powerful than the forces which were seeking to divide the church.

The purpose that God had in mind for them was not fully realized until they found a unity of mutual support and concern in their own fellowship. He was not urging that they all conform to the same pattern of conduct but that they all be the same at the core of their existence.

One of the reasons that we must continue to study the Bible together in the church is that it helps us to a more adequate insight into the nature of the church itself. The opening verses of this particular passage are no exception. It is hardly necessary to point out the divisions and failures of unity in contemporary church life. Most of us are painfully aware of the brokenness in the church. But we are likely to ignore the reality of our life in Christ. Paul's letter helps us to see that more fundamental to our understanding of the church than the weakness and frailty of men are the power and steadfastness of God.

The unity that Paul saw as the consequence of God's saving work in Jesus Christ was not automatic or inevitable. The individual member of the Philippian church had the power to frustrate God's purpose by his own free choice. Therefore, in view of his understanding of what God had done to create unity in the church, Paul called upon the Philippians to avoid acts which opposed God's will and to assume an attitude which conformed to his goals for human life. "Do nothing from selfishness or conceit, but in humility count others better than yourselves" (Philippians 2:3).

There was no thought in Paul's mind that he was exhorting his readers to do the impossible. He knew that some of them had already chosen to do otherwise, but that fact did not throw him into despair. He knew also that the power of God in human life could free a man from selfishness and conceit so that he could humbly place the needs of others before his own. (*S/R*, 63.)

Our tendency in the church today is to set our sights too low. We know that we have done many things from selfishness and conceit; we know also that we have not humbly considered others better than ourselves. In an attempt to be realistic about the possibilities which we have within us, we settle for life as it is. We come to terms with those attitudes and actions which keep us from fulfilling God's purposes for our lives. This is false realism because it denies the presence and power of God in our lives.

PRACTICAL UNITY

The unity that Paul promoted at Philippi was not theoretical but practical. Therefore, he pressed his readers to adopt a general course of action that would enable them to overcome their divisions. "Let each of you look not only to his own interests, but also to the interests of others" (Philippians 2:4). The apostle called them from an exclusive concern for their own needs to an inclusive concern for the needs of others. (*S/R*, 64.) They could not achieve unity by changing a few of the externals of their life together. The price was higher than that; the price was reform and renewal in every phase of their common life.

God intends unity for his people; how can it be achieved? (*S/R*, 65.) The question that Philippians 2:4 poses is: how much are we willing to pay to rid our lives of the divisions that separate us? Unity is no bargain basement transaction. The worst mistake we can make is to think that we can have it on easy terms, with no down payment, and with no re-arrangement of our family budget. If the unity we seek is really God's unity, then we can only have it on God's terms and at the price he has set.

God also demands that we give up the delusion that some-thing done by somebody else in some other place will create unity in the church. The unity that God intends for us in-cludes the whole church at every level and in every place. So regardless of our particular responsibilities we all come under the same demand, and we are judged by the same standard. We must submit every aspect of church life to the rigorous judgment of Paul's exhortation. No matter how dramatic the program or conference or union of denomina-tions may be, if it leaves the church preoccupied with its own interests, nothing has really been changed and the cause of unity has not been advanced. Unity without renewal is a false hope. And renewal without repentance is impossible. Therefore, let each of us look not only to his own interests but also to the interests of others.

HE HUMBLED HIMSELF

Paul's counsel to the Philippians rested upon the life, death, and resurrection of Jesus. The reality of what had been done for them by God was summed up in the ministry of Jesus. The inner attitude of commitment to God and love for each other had been revealed in the life and teaching of Jesus. The true meaning of humility had been set forth in him who did nothing from selfishness or conceit but in all things served others, who had become flesh, who denied himself, and who laid down his life for others. Therefore, Paul gathered up all his counsel to the Philippians in one ringing imperative: "Have this mind among yourselves, which you have in Christ Jesus" (Philippians 2:5).

For Paul there was no command without an accompanying

gift of grace which made it possible, and there was no gift of grace without a corresponding duty or obligation. This balance of grace and commandment, gift and duty is more than a literary device used by Paul to keep his readers interested. It is the rhythm of faith which is absolutely essential for the healthy life of the church. In our own life together in the church we are always in danger of destroying this balance by going to extremes in one direction or another. For example, some of us become so concerned with the demands and duties of church membership that we reduce the good news to a list of rules and regulations which must be carefully observed. Salvation according to this legalistic understanding is doing good things that merit God's favor.

There are others, however, who insist that the grace of God has been given freely: that they are released from all the rules and regulations which have heretofore been marks of the good life. They contend that they have been set free from all external requirements by God's gift of love. Therefore, they say, any attempt to discipline life is a refusal to trust the power of God's action in life. Salvation according to this understanding consists in doing as one pleases to the glory of God. (S/R, 66.)

The way for the church to guard against these preversions of Christian faith is to see that Christ himself is present in the church as both gift and demand. When the church is fully responsive to the presence and power of the risen Lord, she gladly accepts what he offers and she obediently performs what he commands.

One of the means the church employs to maintain the balance of her faithful relationship to Christ is her service of public worship. When the church gathers to celebrate the gospel, she always proclaims what God has done in Christ. She always accepts the obligation to conform her life to what God has revealed in Christ. In her hymns and preaching and sacraments, the church praises God for his great salvation. In her prayers and offerings and service, the church seeks to reproduce in her own life the life of him who is present with her as Lord and Savior.

■ Contrast the views discussed in the preceding paragraphs with the view expressed in *S/R,* 66. How do you understand the freedom of the Christian?

THE MIND OF CHRIST: SERVICE

The divisions that we experience today in the church are evidence that we still need the same basic instruction in the mind of Christ as Paul gave to the Philippians. The "mind of Christ" is not an empty concept into which we may pour whatever strikes our fancy. The mind of Christ is defined for us by the lowly service that Jesus performed as a man among men.

As we read the reports of his ministry in the New Testament, there are certain things that stand out in his life. He possessed unusual powers that he never used to promote his own interests. He never grasped for status or position but always gave himself in service to the needs of others. He accepted the limitations of human life; he claimed nothing for himself that was not given to all other men. It is a fatal error for the church to ignore these characteristic traits of Jesus. The fact that we have ignored them is shown in the claims we make for Jesus and the church. In stubborn disregard of what the New Testament tells us about the life of Jesus, we have claimed for him a position of worldly status which he consistently renounced. We have regarded the church as a center of privilege and prestige for men. The church itself has too often become an arena where men struggle for power and position. (*S/R,* 67 and 68.) The tragedy is that all this has been done in the name of one who took the form of a servant.

■ What evidence do you see that we have attempted to make the church a center of privilege and status? The views of persons outside the church are often enlightening. Have persons in your town or community, who claim to be disillusioned by the church, interviewed on this subject. The results might be more candid if the person conducting the interview is not connected with your class. Let the interviewer, or a member of the class with whom he has talked, share the results of the interview with the class. Discuss: What are some ways the church could and should give up status and privileges in society in order to identify herself with humanity?

■ Related to this subject is the much-discussed question of whether churches should be tax exempt. Four persons, prepared in advance, might form a panel to discuss the pros and cons of this question. Information on the subject may be secured from *S/R,* 67, the public library, an informed lawyer; or your minister might direct you to recent articles dealing with the subject.

■ One form of the struggle for power and position in the church is described in *S/R,* 68. Let one person read it aloud. Discuss together: What attitudes or conditions in local churches might foster this kind of struggle? How do individuals or groups within the church participate in a kind of "buying and selling" of clergy? What forms does the struggle for power and position take among the laity? What practical guidance can be gained from Paul's letter to the Philippian church? (See Philippians 2:1-11.)

Paul understood the cross as the center of Jesus' ministry and the climax of his servant life. This one event more than any other revealed the quality of his life and the core of his being. "And being found in human form he humbled himself and became obedient unto death, even death on a cross" (Philippians 2:8). In this passage Paul was not spinning out a theory but proclaiming an act. From the apostle's point of view, the cross of Jesus was not just an event that happened to a man in Palestine. It was also a style of life that the church was called to manifest as the ruling principle and power of all that she did. Just as Jesus died in obedience to the will of God, so the church was under orders to die in obedience to her Lord.

The plain meaning of what Paul meant when he wrote, "have this mind among yourselves, which you have in Christ

Jesus," was expressed by Jesus when he said, "If any man would come after me, let him deny himself and take up his cross and follow me" (Mark 8:34b). (S/R, 69.)

■ In groups of six to eight persons study Philippians 2:5-8. See both *The New English Bible* and the King James Version as well as a musical adaptation of the passage, "All Praise to Thee, for Thou, O King Divine" (*The Methodist Hymnal*, 74). Use the chart "Study a Portion of the Bible" (Resource Packet, item 2) to guide your study. Discuss your understanding of the passage and its interpretation in this book. Refer to the chart "Biblical Literature" (Resource Packet, item 9) to help you identify the literary form employed in this passage.

In your group define the word *servant* in as many ways as possible. Now, considering your definitions, in what ways is your church a "servant church"? Where in the life of your church, your study group, and yourself do you see humility, obedience, and self-renunciation demonstrated? Where do you sense a lack of these characteristics?

■ Observe a period of silent meditation: According to the interpretation of the preceding paragraphs, the "mind of Christ" is synonymous with the cross. What, then, does seeking the mind of Christ, that is, seeking the way of the cross, mean to you? Read silently S/R, 69.

Consider silently: Suppose you thought of the cross as more than an inspiring decoration in or on the church, or a piece of jewelry, or a bookmark in your Bible? Suppose you took seriously Jesus' words, "Take up your cross and follow me," what changes would you need to make in your life?

In this connection the group might look at the series of cartoons entitled "The Foam Rubber Cross" (Resource Packet, *Man's Search for a Meaningful Faith*, item 11). Consult the Leaders' Guide in that packet for suggestions for using the chart.

All discussions concerning unity in the church miss the real source until they focus upon the cross as the act in which unity is realized. In obedience unto death, "even death on a cross," Jesus renounced selfishness and conceit which separated men from each other and committed himself to the interests of others in an act which bound men together in a perfect union of purpose and deed with the nature and will of God. This means that if we really desire unity in the church today, we must be obedient unto death, "even death on a cross." Selfishness and conceit lie at the root of our separation from each other. The only cure for these fatal diseases is obedience to the will of God which seeks expression in serving the interests of others. The only victory over selfishness and conceit is death, "even death on a cross."

The unity we seek must be God's unity or it is just another proud program that will tear the church apart. God's unity is service that arranges the whole church around the nature and will of God and that commits the whole church to the interests of others. Perhaps the first place to start a movement toward genuine unity in the church is with a serious review of church budgets. The average church budget is an instrument of selfishness and conceit that is used to deny God's will and to avoid every form of sacrificial service. Church budgets often reflect a nominal commitment to the work of God in the world and a fierce determination to look after the interests of the church itself. The result is that the church is separated from God, separated from God's work in the world, and divided within its own membership.

The way out is no mystery. It is the way of Jesus, who "humbled himself and became obedient unto death, even death on a cross." When we organize our resources around the needs of the world, empty ourselves, and take the form of a servant in the world, then we will have this mind among ourselves, which we have in Christ Jesus.

■ What is the relation of the church budget to the kind of unity in the church about which Paul spoke? Study your church budget for this year. The leadership team, or persons assigned the task, should provide mimeographed copies of the budget or should have the information on newsprint for all to see. The report might also include budgets from, perhaps, two previous years. Does your budget affirm or deny the above description of the "average" church budget? Evaluate the concerns of your budget in light of Philippians 2:1-8. How does your budget reflect the concerns of a "servant church"? Have the increases or decreases in your budget over the past few years affected God's work in the world or the interests of the church itself? How do you react to S/R, 14?

Now take this examination one step further; let each person evaluate his own commitment in terms of his financial support to God's work. Check your checkbook.

GOD WITH US—IN SERVICE

The example that Paul set before the Philippians in the life and ministry of Jesus was more than his clever appeal to the virtues of a noble man. Something had happened to Paul and the church which gave to the life of Jesus an authority and power corresponding to the authority and power of God himself. Jesus had been raised from the dead, had appeared to a number of witnesses, and was present in human life as the Lord of the church. It was this experience of the risen Lord that Paul proclaimed when he wrote, "Therefore God has highly exalted him and bestowed on him the name which is above every name" (Philippians 2:9). By losing his life in obedient service to men Jesus had found his life. He did not humble himself in order to qualify for an exalted position. His humility was the highest exaltation possible. It was the way of God among men and, therefore, his life received the approval of God. God had "bestowed on him the name which is above every name." The power of humble ministry in the life of Jesus had triumphed over death itself and was superior to every other force known to men.

There is nothing more powerful than a life of humble service. (S/R, 70.) This is the practical consequence of our faith in the Resurrection. Since God has raised Jesus from the dead, we know that through his risen presence in the church a power is at work in human history that nothing can defeat. Jesus then is more than a pattern for our lives. He is the servant at work in our lives providing guidance, comfort, and strength sufficient for all our needs. We have no reason to be confident about our own ability to triumph over selfishness and conceit and live a life of service for others. But we do not lose hope. Through the power of the Resurrection, which is even now at work within us, we dare to strive to have this mind among ourselves, which was in Christ Jesus. The realism of the good news is not based upon a careful calculation of the possibilities of human life but upon a faithful confession of "the name which is above every name."

In the life, death, and resurrection of Jesus, the servant power of God had overcome the worst that rebellion and unfaithfulness could do. But the victory was not fully realized in human history and could not be until every knee was bowed in submission to Jesus and every tongue confessed that he is Lord. In the power of the Resurrection, Paul witnessed to the Lordship of Jesus Christ in his own life, in the life of the church, and in the world.

■ The importance of humble service is emphasized in John 13:1-17. Let one person read it aloud. Now, listen to an account of servant-hood in the twentieth century (S/R, 70). Perhaps your group would like to attempt a similar ministry. To learn of the kinds of service you might perform, plan a field trip to a deprived area or invite a member of the city council to talk with your group about the needs of persons in your community.

■ Pray together the "Prayer of Saint Francis" (Resource Packet, *Man's Search for a Meaningful Faith,* item 3).

■ Let the leadership team be prepared to give assignments for the next chapter of study and the members of the class be prepared to accept the assignments.

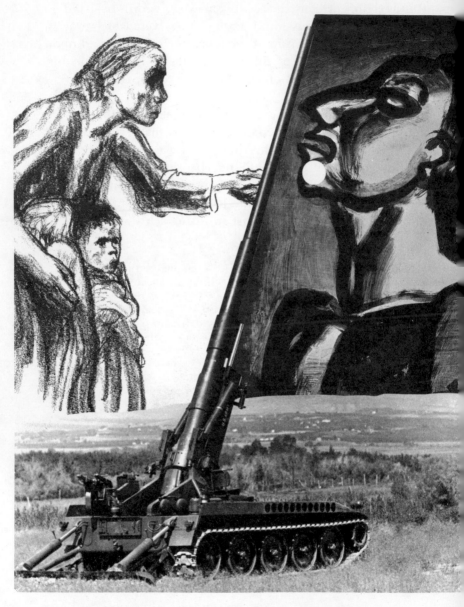

*Has the Church failed to withstand the pressures
of militarism and nationalism?*

9

□□

TELL HIS DISCIPLES AND PETER

Rebellion and unfaithfulness are so firmly entrenched in our lives that no man can save himself. The attraction of false gods and the blindness of men make it impossible for men on the basis of their own strength and insight to establish a saving relationship with the true and living God. This is an emphasis that we resist vigorously.

We resist it because it runs counter to one of the basic assumptions of our age: there is nothing men cannot do by relying on their own industry and knowledge. Self-sufficiency is the first article of our modern creed. If there are areas of our life that have not been brought under control, it is not because we are basically unable to cope with them. It is be-

■ *As you arrive at your place of meeting, check the assignment chart for specific preparation to be made before the session begins.*

■ Set goals for your study of this chapter as suggested on page 17.

cause we have not concentrated our strength and wisdom upon finding a solution. If we really put our hand and heart and mind to the task, there is absolutely nothing we cannot do. So many people today believe.

I am sure that one of the reasons the Bible is not read and studied today is because most people honestly find it difficult to understand its teachings and apply them to our situation. I am equally sure, however, that another reason some of us have given up the study of the Scriptures is simply that we have understood their message and their relevance for our lives, but we stubbornly refuse to hear and heed what they say. (S/R, 71.)

I think this is particularly true of the teaching of the Bible concerning the weakness and frailty of men. There is nothing particularly complicated about the teaching: men refuse the faithful relationship to God that guarantees their well-being; this unfaithfulness corrupts the whole sweep of human existence; men cannot restore the broken relationship with God by their own strength.

If one reads the Bible at all, he is brought face to face with this fundamental insight into the human predicament. So in order to avoid coming to grips with what the Bible teaches about man's life before God, one simply gives up reading the Bible. The fact that the Bible is not read and studied in the church may be more than a sign of indifference. It may also be a deliberate act of unfaithfulness. (S/R, 72.)

I WILL NOT DENY YOU

The figure upon whom we will concentrate our attention as we study Mark 14:26-72 and 16:1-8 is Peter. He is the chief spokesman in Mark 14:26-31. In 14:32-42 Jesus makes special mention of his name. And in 14:53-72 Peter is the only one of the disciples who is close enough to be involved in Jesus' trial by the Jerusalem council. And finally at the empty tomb the heavenly messenger singles out Peter by name and directs the women to tell him of the Resurrection.

Why did the author of Mark give Peter such a prominent place in the death and resurrection of Jesus? Perhaps we can never know precisely what was the author's purpose in giving Peter such a prominent place in these narratives of the suffering and resurrection of our Lord. This suggests that we ought not to approach them as sources of information about an ancient historical figure but rather we should listen to them as means through which God tells us about himself and our relationship to him. What we read and study about Peter has no value until it becomes a means of helping us to understand our own involvement in the crucifixion and resurrection of our Lord. (*S/R*, 73 and 74.)

■ Use *S/R*, 73 and 74. Let one person read the major portion of *S/R*, 73, and two persons alternate reading the list of concerns. Then let five persons act out *S/R*, 74. Then let all group members personally work on the following scale of involvement:

Jesus said, "What you do to one of the least, you do to me." Assuming this applies to crucifixion as much as to giving a cup of cold water, *do you think the following are ways we crucify Jesus today?* That is, am I helping to crucify Jesus if I—

	Yes	Maybe	No
(1) hold attitudes that lead to war	___	___	___
(2) refuse to sell a house to a minority group member	___	___	___
(3) try to subvert a labor union	___	___	___
(4) steal from my employer	___	___	___
(5) kill or injure a person by careless driving or drunken driving	___	___	___
(6) destroy a marriage by unfaithfulness or neglect	___	___	___
(7) make my child feel unwanted or worthless	___	___	___

133

	Yes	Maybe	No
(8) refuse to support my minister on crucial social issues	____	____	____
(9) criticize my husband or wife for spending too much time in community service	____	____	____

Discuss your reactions to these possibilities.

■ Use the chart "Study a Portion of the Bible" (Resource Packet, item 2, procedure 3) with the Scripture for this chapter, Mark 14:26-72; 16:1-8. See the Leaders' Guide in the packet.

The risen Lord had no illusions about those whom he had chosen to be with him and share his work. "And Jesus said to them, 'You will all fall away; for it is written, "I will strike the shepherd, and the sheep will be scattered"'" (Mark 14:27; read Zechariah 13:7). The disciples did indeed fall away. In times of persecution the church was frequently unable to hold together, and her members scattered like sheep without a shepherd. The power of the Resurrection had not taken the church out of the world nor had it given the church the strength to stand firm against her foes. Just as Jesus had been deserted in his lifetime by his followers, so the risen Lord was deserted by those whom he blessed with his presence in the church.

Peter speaks for and foreshadows the church. One of the last things the church held onto was the belief that she could stand the test and not desert her Lord. The church refused to know herself as she was known, so the author had her speak through Peter to protest her loyalty. "Peter said to him, 'Even though they all fall away, I will not'" (Mark 14:29). How far this was from the truth about the church was revealed in Jesus' reply, "Truly, I say to you, this very night, before the cock crows twice, you will deny me three times" (Mark 14:30). The possibility of betrayal in the church would not come in some remote hour of testing; it would come suddenly in the immediate demand of faithful-

134

ness and would just as suddenly reveal the failure of the church.

THE STORY OF FAILURE

As we examine our own life together in the church in the light of this passage, we know that our fellowship is a continuing sign of God's gracious favor. Through the presence of the risen Lord, we have been chosen and equipped for God's work of service in the world. When we gather in our congregations for worship and depart for ministry, we do so because we are called by Christ's grace and commissioned to do his will. All attempts to account for the life of the church on the basis of human relationships and humanitarian concerns fail to reckon with the fact that we are bound to each other by our experience of a common Lord. (*S/R,* 75.) They also fail to understand that our ministry in the world is based upon the revelation of God's nature and purpose in the life, death, and resurrection of our Lord Jesus Christ.

This high view of the church does not mean that the church is able to remain faithful to her nature and calling. Her history is a story of repeated failure to remain true to her Lord in times of persecution and testing. This is not something which the world says about the church or which we confess to each other in the church. It is what we see about ourselves when the risen Lord discloses himself to us. *For example, in our time the Lord discloses himself as the Prince of Peace, but the church has not withstood the excesses of militarism and nationalism.* As the pressures mount in our society to bring every institution into support of a policy of violence and force, the cause of peace finds fewer and fewer supporters in the church. (*S/R,* 76.)

■ See *S/R,* 76. Discuss: In the cartoon, are the women reacting against the "Peace" sign or the beard? How are our attitudes toward a point of view influenced by how nearly its supporters act and look like us?

As I ponder the full impact of what I have just written, I find myself seeking to find some way to soften the blow. The temptation to qualify our failures and establish conditions that are favorable to us is one that is particularly powerful for those of us who have tried to do right and have made a commitment to the church. I am no more ready than Peter to accept the judgment of the Lord upon my loyalty and dedication. So I join with him in protesting, "Even though they all fall away, I will not." What an attractive fantasy that is! All the world fleeing in the moment of trial but I standing alone in courageous devotion to my Lord. But it is a fantasy with no foundation in reality. The risen Lord does not base his relationship to me upon my imagined ability to stand up to the test.

We stand condemned in his presence by the anxiety of our manner and by the very words which we speak. We do not know ourselves because we do not know him. In all his dealings with us he has shown that his way is the way of obedience unto death, "even death on a cross" (Philippians 2:8), yet we continue to harbor the notion that there is another way for us which would enable us to be with him. The fact that we say, "*if* I must die with you," is evidence that we have already rejected his life of service in the world. All that remains is the specific hour of testing which will bring to light the acts of denial which lie hidden in our hearts. Let no man assume that he or his group is not included in the sweeping and penetrating indictment of this passage. In the shadow of the cross there is no righteous remnant. There are only weak and needy men who in the attempt to deny their guilt and justify themselves all say the same thing: "If I must die with you, I will not deny you."

THE FLESH IS WEAK

The writer of Mark turned next to show how the failure expressed itself in specific acts of denial. The scenes are familiar: Jesus' agony in Gethsemane, Judas' act of betrayal, and Peter's denial of his Lord in the courtyard of the high priest. These scenes were used to present a consistent picture of the risen Lord. In all of them the Lord of the church was portrayed in complete charge of what happens. He was not torn by doubt or troubled by indecision. His enemies and his friends were set over against him as examples of the impotence and unfaithfulness of men. He alone was faithful and all that he suffered at the hands of men was the result of his obedience to the will of his Father.

The event in the garden of Gethsemane showed that the church failed to see the precariousness of her situation and to trust completely in God. The church was complacent in the presence of danger and therefore confident that her own strength was sufficient. In the opening words of Jesus to his disciples, his appraisal of the situation was contrasted with theirs. He said to them, "Sit here, while I pray" (Mark 14:32b). God's work in the world was always under attack, but through prayer his power was available to those committed to his will. While the disciples were content to sit, the Lord of the church was greatly troubled and distressed. The one thing they needed most was to be aware of the danger of unfaithfulness and to keep alert. "And he said to them, 'My soul is very sorrowful, even to death; remain here, and watch'" (Mark 14:34). (S/R, 77.)

In contrast, those whom the Lord had taken with him were unaware of their time of testing. "And he came and found them sleeping, and he said to Peter, 'Simon, are you asleep? Could you not watch one hour? Watch and pray that you may not enter into temptation; the spirit indeed is willing, but the flesh is weak'" (Mark 14:37-38). Simon Peter was singled out here, because he was representative of the church. The complacence of the church was not a momentary lapse

137

but a characteristic condition. As often as the Lord appeared to the church, he found her sleeping and taking her rest (Mark 14:39-41a).

Just as the historical Jesus had been rejected and deserted, so the risen Lord suffers, alone and despised in the world. "It is enough; the hour has come; the Son of man is betrayed into the hands of sinners. Rise, let us be going; see, my betrayer is at hand" (Mark 14:41b-42).

The connecting link between our present situation and Gethsemane is not our ability to turn the clock back but the presence of the risen Lord in our lives. Wherever Christians are faithful in their encounters in the world, there will always be resistance. God prepares us for this resistance.

The one thing needful as we enter our hour of testing is prayer. Prayer in this context is not a matter of offering words to God; it is presenting our lives to God in the confidence that he alone can give us the strength and guidance we need. (S/R, 78.) We are so blind and insensitive to the threat of unfaithfulness that we see no need for strength other than our own. Even as our Lord gathers us around him, we fall away from him.

The good news proclaimed by the author of Mark in this narrative is that while the church sleeps and takes her rest, the Lord of the church watches and prays. In him the willing spirit overcomes the weakness of the flesh. His lordship is expressed in the fact that he gives himself for the weak, suffers at the hands of sinners, and submits to the humiliation of betrayal.

■ Conduct a panel discussion on the following bases: (1) Compare *S/R,* 78 and First Peter with the above interpretation of Gethsemane (page 137). (2) How is the Lordship of Jesus being expressed today? (3) What are some examples of attacks on those attempting to be faithful in the world of today? (4) Why do some people charge the church or its individual members with communist sympathies when they work for social justice for all people?

Judas' betrayal emphasizes the fact that the Lord of the church was handed over to sinners by one of the disciples—by the church itself. "And immediately, while he was still speaking, Judas came, one of the twelve, and with him a crowd with swords and clubs, from the chief priests and the scribes and elders" (Mark 14:43). The betrayal was a subtle thing. It gave the appearance of affection and adoration, but it was a public act of rejection of all that the Lord did and was. "Now the betrayer had given them a sign, saying, 'The one I shall kiss is the man; seize him and lead him away safely.' And when he came, he went up to him at once, and said, 'Master!' And he kissed him. And they laid hands on him and seized him" (Mark 14:44-46).

REBELLION AGAINST GOD

This betrayal is repeated wherever the risen Lord is present in human history. He still comes claiming the kingdoms of this world as the kingdom of his Father. And in his risen presence he brings to light the rebellion against God that is characteristic of men and their institutions. There is no aspect of his Spirit that does not conflict with the sin in us men and our ways. Take love, for instance. In him love is active good will that excludes no one, not even the enemy. But the world correctly sees that this kind of love undermines all that it had understood by the word. So the Spirit of the Lord is opposed by the institutions of men and the church is faced with a moment of testing. Will the church follow the Lord or the world? The answer is given in the deeds of the church, in acts of cruelty, and in official programs of persecution. The church has hated its enemies and in the act has joined those who come with swords and clubs to capture the Lord. There are not many instances of those who took the cross to follow him. (S/R, 79.)

■ Divide the group into two teams: one to *uphold* and one to *deny* the charge in the preceding paragraphs and S/R, 79—that the church has betrayed Christ. Ask *each* team to give *evidence* for its position, regardless of personal opinion or feeling. List and then discuss these points.

The final act of betrayal was done in the courtyard of the high priest. Again let us keep in mind that although the writer drew upon the tradition concerning Jesus' last days on earth (about A.D. 30) , he was also writing from the point of view of his own experience of the risen Lord (35 or 40 years later) . His major concern, therefore, was not to record what happened in the past but to witness to the living faith of the church. We should approach this narrative as a description of the relationship of the church to her Lord.

Once more Peter appears as a representative of the church. From a safe distance, he had followed Jesus from Gethsemane, "right into the courtyard of the high priest; and he was sitting with the guards, and warming himself at the fire" (Mark 14:54) . Peter was so near and yet so far away from his Lord. What separated them? Just one thing: Peter was determined to save himself, but Jesus was committed to doing the will of God. As Mark described the course of the trial in the council chamber, the purpose foremost in his mind was to proclaim the glory of the risen Lord.

The basic contrast was not between the Lord and the religious authorities but between him and Peter. The Lord had remained dumb before his accusers and had spoken only to answer a question that was to cost him his life. Peter, on the other hand, defended himself from start to finish. One of the serving maids saw him warming himself in the courtyard, and said, "You also were with the Nazarene, Jesus" (see Mark 14:66-67) . He sensed his danger at once and seeking to save his life he said, "I neither know nor understand what you mean" (Mark 14:68*a*) . She followed him outside the gate, and said to the bystanders, "This man is one of them" (Mark 14:69) . He denied it again. But after a little

140

while the bystanders said to him: "Certainly you are one of them; for you are a Galilean" (Mark 14:70). And this time he invoked a curse on himself and swore, "I do not know this man of whom you speak" (Mark 14:71). Then the cock crew a second time and Peter remembered that the Lord had predicted his failure. "And he broke down and wept" (Mark 14:72).

The only relationship possible between the Lord who gave himself without condition and Peter who sought desperately to save himself was repentance. To have been aware of the Lord's presence was to break down and weep, because he had been denied not once, but repeatedly.

Where are we in relationship to him? Always at a safe distance! When the world takes our profession seriously and identifies us with him, we show how far away we really are. (S/R, 80.) We deny him, not once but habitually. The opportunities to join him in giving our lives in self-denying service in the world come over and over again. Many of these require that we die with him. So we say that we have never known him. We concentrate all our energies on defending ourselves. We seek to save our lives, and we succeed only in losing them. The new day that our Lord's presence promised is transformed by our unfaithfulness into the same old time of self-seeking and failure. He remains with us, but now his presence is judgment. The only way for us to acknowledge that he is here is to break down and weep in repentance. "The spirit indeed is willing, but the flesh is weak" (Matthew 26:41).

■ Read S/R, 80. In small groups discuss: What are some causes of this kind of attitude? If the majority of us (church members) are motivated by the desire to achieve success, and young ministers are from our own families, why should we expect their motives to be different from ours?

■ Display the picture "Christ and Missile" (Resource Packet, item 6). Let one person read aloud S/R, 82; then all sing S/R, 81.

HE HAS RISEN, HE IS NOT HERE

Through these narratives that focus upon the figure of Peter, the author of Mark presented a picture of the life of the church that has lasting significance. But he did not stop with the unfaithfulness and failure that the risen Lord always encountered not only in the world but also in the church. He sought also to proclaim the good news that sustained the church in her hour of failure and that gave her life and mission. This he did by showing how the failures of men provided the setting for God's victory in Christ. He did not attempt to avoid the awful result of man's betrayal. The suffering and death of Jesus were real. (S/R, 81 and 82.) The risen Lord was one who had died. Those who rejected him in his risen life could have him with them again only as they received him from the grave. This then is the climax of the good news proclaimed by the author of Mark: The risen Lord leaves the tomb and offers to men that which they are unable to secure for themselves, forgiveness of their sins. How he understood this gospel is revealed to us in his witness to the Resurrection in Mark 16:1-8.

Much of what we do in the church that has the appearance of devotion and worship is in reality the funeral ritual that we conduct for one whom we admired but who we now believe is powerless in the grave. On a typical Sunday morning is there any more faith in the world than there was that first day of the week centuries ago when three women went to the tomb? If the power of the Resurrection is to be measured by the yardstick of our faith, then it is not good news but the bad news of yet another human failure.

The church persists in human history because of the power of the Resurrection. Unfaithfulness is not final. This is our experience. The witness of the author of Mark is our witness. What we cannot do for ourselves God has done for us. The stone has been rolled away. The good news of the triumph of Jesus Christ has been announced to us, and we have believed. He is not here in the tomb of our denial and betrayal. He is always there before us ministering to our needs and giving himself in unfailing love.

Without him, we could never have won our way back to God or into his kingdom. But he has come to us in our rebellion and disobedience and made our life east of Eden the place of his gracious presence. The promise of Immanuel —*God with us*—is fulfilled in God's good news: "He has risen, he is not here; see the place where they laid him. But go, tell his disciples and Peter that he is going before you to Galilee; there you will see him, as he told you."

Now, as in the first century, the experience of God's good news is an awe-inspiring event. One of the tests of the effectiveness of our reading the Scriptures and our hearing the gospel is how they make us aware of the power and presence of God in our lives. If there is no trembling, no astonishment, no reverent fear, it may be a sign that we have hardened our hearts to the reality of God with us.

■ Use the chart "The Bible Is Not: The Bible Is" (Resource Packet, item 10) . See the Leaders' Guide in the packet for suggestions for its use. As a result of this discussion, how nearly does your view of the Bible agree with that described on the chart?
■ Let all who will tell of any experience of "God with us" coming from their study of the Bible or from hearing the gospel.
■ Close with silence.
■ Let the leadership team be prepared to make assignments for the next chapter of study and the members of the group be prepared to accept the assignments.

Can Christ set us free?

10

□□

THE HELP THAT COMES FROM GOD

"You can't change human nature." How often we have said this ourselves or heard it said by others! It is a widespread assumption about the human condition and one that is hardly ever questioned. Why is it so readily accepted? Perhaps the chief reason is that it is a comfortable and re assuring word of support to those of us who are content to settle with things as they are. (*S/R*, 83.) If human nature cannot really be changed, then there is no reason for one to waste his time and energy trying. What an easy way to excuse all our own shortcomings!

The assumption that human nature cannot be changed is also a form of resignation to the bondage of the past. That

■ *As you arrive at your place of meeting, check the assignment chart for specific preparation to be made before the session begins.*

■ Set goals for your study of this chapter as suggested on page 17.

is, if we can discover what a man has been in the past, then we can know what he is now and we can predict what he will be in the future. The cruelty of this attitude toward others is illustrated over and over again in the refusal of our society to believe that a criminal can ever become anything except what he has been. *(S/R, 84.)*

This assumption that men are chained to their past also plays a decisive part in most forms of social, cultural, and racial discrimination. The continued segregation of the Negro in white Western civilization is at least in part a refusal of some people in the white community to believe that the Negro can ever be anything except a black savage. Most forms of injustice and denial of basic rights to the poor are based upon the conviction that because a man was born in poverty and ignorance he is consigned to that condition forever.

Some of the policies which have been adopted in our educational institutions reflect this same fatalistic assumption about the finality of a man's past. For example, we know now that practically all intelligence tests are tests of how one has been encouraged to take advantage of opportunities to learn. If the encouragement has been lacking and the opportunities limited, then the individual will score poorly on tests. How have these tests been used? All too often they have been the basis of deciding that an individual lacks the ability to learn and that he should be denied further opportunities to learn or assigned to courses which are within his "capacity." Thus education, which ought to be the means of exploring the present and unlocking the future, has become an instrument of enslavement to the unalterable past.

One result of taking history (the past) seriously is the conclusion that we cannot tear ourselves loose from our past. When we review our own personal histories, we are shocked to discover that we tend to keep on in the same old rut. *(S/R, 85.)* Likewise, when we examine the history of our nation and our world, we cannot fail to be impressed with how we keep on repeating the mistakes of the past. The bondage of the past is not imagined but very real.

■ What false assumptions may underlie our desire and efforts to maintain the status quo?

Invite one or two young persons to come to your class to sing (or read) and interpret the song, "The Times They Are A-Changin'" by Bob Dylan. Or a member of your group might read the words aloud. Allow time for group members to ask questions.

Then discuss in total group: What conditions or situations contribute to the urgency of changing times? Was the same degree of urgency felt a generation or two ago? Why? Why not? Why are adults reluctant to admit that the past is gone? What results when persons are not willing to respond positively to "changing times"? Contrast the attitudes toward change today with those expressed in the gospel song, "The Old-Time Religion." What differences in mood and outlook on life do you detect? The songs mentioned above are available as recordings. Further information can be obtained from any music store.

■ Or brainstorm, as quickly as ideas can be listed on chalkboard or newsprint, the traits (inadequacies) of human nature that we cite to convince ourselves that human nature cannot be changed.

■ Let individuals cite examples to prove or disprove the idea that society does not allow a man to forget, be forgiven of, or rise above his past.

This position can be maintained only by closing one's mind to the witness of those who testify that their lives *have been* changed and that the course of history has been altered. In a sense, the entire Bible is a book of testimony to the power at work in the lives of men and nations, a power that has freed them from the bondage of the past. The good news is that what *has been* is not necessarily what *will be*. The biblical witness is united in affirming that God is with us in the present moment, striking away the shackles of what we have been and offering the freedom of what we shall be.

Because God is at work in our lives, we are called to oppose the fatalistic assumption that human nature cannot be changed. We have no choice here. If we are to be faithful to the God of Abraham, Isaac, and Jacob, the God of our Lord and Savior Jesus Christ, then we must renounce the complacent acceptance of life as it is and affirm the freedom for the future which his presence makes possible.

One of the most powerful witnesses to God's work in changing human nature is the report of the conversion of Paul in the Book of Acts. Luke has reported this event three times in Acts (9:1-19; 22:1-21; 26:1-23). Any one of these narratives would reward our study at this point, but I have chosen the last one (Acts 26:1-23) because it raises the problem of bondage to the past and proclaims that the Resurrection is God's solution to that problem.

How can study of the Bible help us see the forces that shut us up in the "prison house" of the past? How can we experience the power of the Resurrection that opens the door to what we can become?

■ In small groups compare biblical accounts of persons who were able to break with their past and those who remained bound to their past: Matthew 19:16-22; Luke 9:57-62; Luke 19:1-10; John 3:1-21; John 4:7-30; Acts 26:1-23. What aspects of the past did they have to break with? What was there about an encounter with Jesus that gave them the power or motivation to be released from their past? Why were some unable to break with their past?

■ Display the picture "Man in a Cage" (Resource Packet, *Man's Search for a Meaningful Faith,* item 12). Familiar lines from a poem say, "Self is the only prison that can ever bind the soul." *

What forces, habits, ideas, attitudes, traditions imprison us? What is the relation of the self to these? How may the knowledge of God's presence release us from each of these? See the Leaders' Guide in the packet mentioned above for further directions for studying the picture.

I HAVE LIVED AS A PHARISEE

The history of the first decades of the growth of the Christian church was a history of conflict. One of the points of conflict was the Jewish opposition to the expansion of the

church in Gentile territory. One of the reasons Luke wrote
Acts was to explain the Gentile mission and to defend the
church against the charges that were being made against her
by the Jews. In the speech that Paul was reported to have
made before King Agrippa, we hear not only Paul's defense
but Luke's defense of the church against her critics. The
Christian church had broken out of the old Jewish patterns
of separation and discrimination. What was her ground for
this radical break with the past? How did the church interpret this break so that others would not only be sympathetic
but would join in her mission in the world?

Paul began his defense by acknowledging his Jewish past.
"My manner of life from my youth, spent from the beginning among my own nation and at Jerusalem, is known by
all the Jews" (Acts 26:4). These words made it clear that
Paul had nothing to hide in his past. He assumed that what
he had been as a Jew was fully acceptable to the Jewish
authorities and the civil rulers alike. How completely he had
broken with that past was expressed in the calm manner
he could speak about it. The very fact that he no longer felt
compelled either to defend or attack it indicated that he had
been released from it.

As Luke developed this narrative, he went on to describe
how Paul had made a decision about what kind of Jew he
would be. "They have known for a long time, if they are
willing to testify, that according to the strictest party of our
religion I have lived as a Pharisee" (Acts 26:5). The Jews
had accused Paul of defiling the temple by bringing a Greek
into it (Acts 21:27-36). His defense was to call attention to
his reputation for strict obedience to the letter of the law.
He had been more exact than an ordinary practitioner of the
Jewish religion. He had attracted attention by submitting
to the most rigorous demands of the law and by fulfilling
them down to the smallest detail. But it no longer represent-

ed the meaning and purpose of his existence. Something had happened to him that had set him free, even from his good reputation as a superior Pharisee.

The power that had released Paul from his past and enabled him to accept it was not wholly unrelated to what he had been. His past was not godless. In being faithful to his present experience of the power of God, he saw that the same power had been at work in his Jewish heritage.

MEN WITHOUT HOPE

In all of this Luke was building to the climax of his argument. What was at stake was not Paul's good reputation as a Jew or his outstanding achievements as a strict Pharisee. The issue was really the sovereign power of God. The experience of God's power had freed Paul from his past and had opened before him the unexplored future of life lived in absolute dependence upon that power.

If a person draws a line at any point in human experience and says that God's power does not extend beyond that line, then he has limited God, and he has confessed that he does not really trust God. The point where men are most likely to prove unfaithful is death. Here all God's promises meet their ultimate test. Unless hope extends to the grave and beyond, then it is a blind alley that leads only to frustration and despair. (*S/R*, 86.)

Paul's experience of God's power had enabled him to affirm that there were no limits to God's sovereignty, not even death. And on the strength of that experience, he suddenly shifted from a defense of his faith to an offensive against the unfaithfulness of men living without hope. The question that had to be answered was not why he lived in hope but why his accusers had renounced hope. They were on trial, not he! "Why is it thought incredible by any of you that God raises the dead?" (Acts 26:8) . (*S/R*, 87.)

One of the most persistent forms of the unfaithful denial

of God's power and presence in the world is the attempt to limit his activity in terms of some past experience. Our study of the Scriptures is always in danger of becoming an unfaithful worship of the past unless it helps us to come face to face with the living God who is greater than any gift of insight that we have received from him. There is a continuous struggle in the church between those who follow the promise of God wherever it leads and those who seek to call a halt in the pilgrimage at some point of personal or group achievement.

■ Do we follow God faithfully wherever he leads, or do we turn aside or stop at points of personal or group achievement? Discuss: How, if at all, is personal faith affected by the acquiring of knowledge, increasing financial security, or social success? Use the Christian Group Life Check List (Resource Packet, *Man's Search for a Meaningful Faith,* item 16) to evaluate the openness of your group to continued seeking and learning. The Leaders' Guide in that packet provides directions for using the chart.

The opening verses of this narrative confront us with one of the fundamental issues of Christian faith. What is at stake is not the glory and fame of the church as a religious institution but its very existence as the faithful people of God. The basic requirement of the people of God is absolute and unlimited trust in the sovereignty of God. Where can the church draw the line and say that beyond this point there is no hope? The answer of Luke in this speech ascribed to Paul is that no lines may be drawn. The future is absolutely open.

IN RAGING FURY AGAINST THEM

For Luke, the key to understanding the power of God that triumphed over death itself was the life of Jesus of Nazareth. It was through his relationship to Jesus that Paul had experienced the power of the Resurrection. (Paul did not know Jesus during his earthly ministry. He had learned

151

about him through contact with the church and through his experience of the risen Lord.) Therefore, Paul's freedom from the past had to be understood as something that had been given to him by the Lord. If men persisted in believing it was incredible that God raises the dead, it was because they opposed Jesus. So the first thing to do in combating their unfaithfulness was to show how the wrong attitude toward Jesus had been overcome in Paul's life. Luke began by referring to Paul's zealous and conscientious opposition to Jesus. "I myself was convinced that I ought to do many things in opposing the name of Jesus of Nazareth" (Acts 26:9).

As we attempt to relate Acts 26:9 to our present situation, the most important words to keep in mind are "the name of Jesus of Nazareth." The name or the power of Jesus is the power released in human history by absolute dependence upon the power and presence of God. The fate of this power in the world is the same in every age: it is opposed by those who wish to exert their own power and depend on their own achievements. Perhaps it is not openly announced or admitted, but many of us today believe that any power that might free men from the bondage of dependence upon themselves and their own works ought to be opposed. Many people feel independent; they have a great faith in their own works. They are against any acknowledgment that their power and their works are not all-sufficient.

For example, in the field of criminology the whole concept of capital punishment has been examined very carefully and generally rejected as having no positive value in our society. Yet in the name of justice and the desire for revenge and under the guise of respect for law and order, we continue to execute fellow human beings because they have been found guilty of certain crimes. It is one means by which we may exert our own power for, after all, what power could be greater than that of legally taking the life of another?

This law of the jungle is questioned and judged by Jesus of Nazareth. The life of Jesus declares that there are no limits to the power of God's love, that even a murderer is included in that love. But we do not trust God's power so we resort to our own power to protect our own achievements. If a man is dangerous to the point of being a threat to our lives, we feel justified in invoking the power of the state to get rid of that threat by killing the man. We defend this barbarism by appealing to the past: our past and the past of the one executed. Society has always killed its enemies, and this man deserved to die because he had acted as an enemy. Thus, the name of Jesus of Nazareth is opposed today. *(S/R, 88.)*

■ How far are we willing to trust the power of God's love?

After reading the above discussion, try an opinion poll. Indicate your personal opinion by checking the statements you agree with:

_____ Capital punishment is immoral.

_____ The death penalty is a just and moral punishment for major crimes of violence.

_____ The death penalty is ineffective as a deterrent to violent crime.

_____ Capital punishment does act as a deterrent to violent crime.

_____ Capital punishment is unfair and discriminatory.

_____ Capital punishment is fair when administered fairly.

_____ It is the inequities that should be abolished, not the penalty itself.

A panel of four persons, prepared in advance, may discuss the pros and cons of capital punishment in the light of the claim that it opposes the power of God's love as seen in Jesus of Nazareth. They may consult the minister, the public library, encyclopedias, *Doctrines and Discipline of The Methodist Church,* and *S/R,* 88, for information. Also consult a lawyer or judge who can supply information on the status of the law regarding capital punishment in your state. Allow time after the panel discussion for any members of the group to change, present, or defend their opinion.

I AM JESUS WHOM YOU ARE PERSECUTING

Luke understood that the power of the Resurrection which liberated Paul from his past was experienced by Paul in the context of conflict with the church. Paul did not deliberately set out to change his own life. Rather, he threw himelf whole-heartedly into the battle against those whose faith challenged all that he was and did. "Thus I journeyed to Damascus with the authority and commission of the chief priests" (Acts 26:12). Yet even as he traveled that road in devotion to his past he was exposed to a power and presence that would set him on another road and give him another object of devotion. "At mid-day, O king, I saw on the way a light from heaven, brighter than the sun, shining round me and those who journeyed with me" (Acts 26:13).

Here Luke used the traditional language of revelation to emphasize that Paul was the object of action which could be explained only as the power and presence of God. All the apostle's faculties were engaged by what took place, but the source of action lay outside his own life in the will and de-sire of another. He was not left to puzzle over the identity of that other presence but received an explanation of what had happened to him. "And when we had all fallen to the ground, I heard a voice saying to me in the Hebrew language, 'Saul, Saul, why do you persecute me? It hurts you to kick against the goads'" (Acts 26:14).

Paul was told that in opposing God's faithful people on earth he was opposing God himself. God was not confined to the temple or locked in the sacred events of the past. He was present throughout the land with the faithful followers of Jesus, and he was encountered in the events that were un-folding in the present moment.

There is good news here for us. The good news is not that we have to free ourselves from our past and find a new center for our lives. Any man who has ever set out to do that on his own strength has found that it leads finally to frustration and failure. The good news is that even when we hurl our-selves in our unfaithfulness into the battle against God's faithful people, there God himself is present with us—even when we are opposing his will. So he was with Paul. God is at work in the world disclosing himself to us through the life of those whom we persecute or abuse. (S/R, 89 and 90.) His power focuses on us to change us from what we are to what we ought to be.

The power of God is not restricted to some sacred sphere; it breaks full upon us in those places where we set ourselves against him. The good news is that he cares enough to judge our past and to upset our convictions about what we are and do. When we lash out in self-righteous anger against those whose faithfulness questions our unfaithfulness, we reveal that the voice of God has been heard in our conscience. For example, the majority of the members of our churches have resisted and opposed those who have renounced war as a means of settling international disputes. Yet even as the majority has condemned the pacifist minority, the troubled conscience of men of violence has been revealed. It still hurts to kick against the goads.

■ Leadership team will display the picture "Negro Woman" (Resource Packet, *Man's Search for a Meaningful Faith*, item 9). Study the picture while one person reads slowly S/R, 89. Discuss: What are you, as an individual, a class, or a church, doing that would offer hope to this woman? What is the motivation for the service you are giving? How do you determine priorities for the nature and extent of your service? The Leaders' Guide in the packet mentioned above will suggest further questions for discussion.

Where in the world may we affirm the power and presence of God today? The answer suggested by this Scripture narrative is that he is to be found with the saints in prison or condemned to die, with those who are punished and persecuted for righteousness' sake. In the contemporary experience of God's action, we are more likely to oppose him rather than support him. Those upon whom we unleash our raging fury are likely to be the bone and muscle and nerve of the risen Lord. Their suffering and death confront us with the power of the Resurrection which may open our eyes so that we may see the light from heaven and which may unstop our ears that we may hear the word of our salvation.

The faithful who die daily are the powerful instruments through whom God has chosen to change our human nature, to conquer our past and set us free. The good news is that the risen Lord is there with those whom we persecute, and through their suffering he makes us aware of his saving presence with us. From the dumb faces of all his hurt children he asks, "Why do you persecute me?" In trembling recognition we answer, "Who are you, Lord?" And still the Lord replies, "I am Jesus whom you are persecuting." The prison house of our past is unlocked by the revelation that Jesus the crucified is the risen Lord. Because the Lord Jesus Christ still suffers and dies with those who bear the mark of pain the light still shines round us and a voice is heard. (*S/R*, 90.)

> ■ Divide your group into three study groups; if you have a large class, more than one group may work on the same assignment.
> Each group will read Acts 26:4-15, giving special attention to verses 9 through 15. Then Group A will read *S/R*, 90; Group B will read *S/R*, 91; and Group C will read *S/R*, 92. Discuss these questions: What is the nature of the persecution described in the reading? What comparable situation exists within your area of influence? How do the words *I am Jesus whom you are persecuting* apply to the situation? What response is required of you?

As the result of Paul's experience of the risen Lord in the martyrdom of the church, he was called to serve and witness. The good news that freed him from his past also claimed him for the future.

> "Rise and stand upon your feet; for I have appeared to you for this purpose, to appoint you to serve and bear witness to the things in which you have seen me and to those in which I will appear to you, delivering you from the people and from the Gentiles—to

whom I send you to open their eyes, that they may turn from darkness to light and from the power of Satan to God, that they may receive forgiveness of sins and a place among those who are sanctified by faith in me" (Acts 26:16-18).

Our own experiences of the Resurrection have the same purpose. God has raised Jesus from the grave and sent him to us as our risen Lord so that we might become instruments of his work in the world. The gift of his gracious presence places us under obligation to tell the world what has happened to us. We cannot receive God's blessing without at the same time accepting his appointment to serve and bear witness. He always comes to us in our need, in our bondage and blindness.

I STAND HERE TESTIFYING

The result of Paul's experience of the risen Lord was his life of obedient service. As he stood before King Agrippa in Caesarea, he summarized his whole life from the Damascus road encounter down to that very moment as the fulfillment of the Lord's commandment. "Wherefore, O King Agrippa, I was not disobedient to the heavenly vision, but declared first to those at Damascus, then at Jerusalem and throughout all the country of Judea, and also to the Gentiles, that they should repent and turn to God and perform deeds worthy of their repentance" (Acts 26:19-20).

The most important factor in understanding what Paul had become was not his relationship to any human group or institution but his obedience to God's will. (S/R, 92.) His life had found a new direction and that fact was showed in his service to all whom he met in Damascus, Jerusalem, throughout all Judea, and among the Gentiles. This summary of the scope of his ministry indicated that what had been announced concerning God's purpose had been realized in his life.

The walls of separation had been broken down by the risen Lord and Paul had passed through the openings to declare the good news. Another sign of this was the message he declared. It was the same for Jew and Gentile alike. The power of the Resurrection had turned Paul around, had made him do an about face, and his new life of service was begun. He proclaimed the same power to Jews and Gentiles without distinction. He saw *all* men in rebellion against God, in bondage to their past. He offered *all* men the power that enabled them to turn toward God and find release from what they had been and done. Because his life had been freed for service, he declared that the destiny of all men was to "perform deeds worthy of repentance," that is, to reveal that they had turned to God by serving each other in love.

Paul encountered difficulties and opposition in his ministry, not because he was unskilled in human relations but because he was faithful to God. "For this reason the Jews seized me in the temple and tried to kill me" (Acts 26:21). "For this reason" refers to his obedience to the heavenly vision. The Jews had charged him with breaking the law of God and defiling the temple. Why had they made the charge? Because they wanted to silence this voice which called them to turn from their idolatrous devotion to the past to serve the true and living God.

What enabled Paul to withstand the fierce opposition of unfaithful men? It was neither his own courage nor his own strength but the power of the Resurrection. "To this day I have had the help that comes from God" (Acts 26:22a). God was not only present in human history but he was also actively engaged in helping those who sought obediently to do his will. Paul was not alone; therefore, he was able to stand the test of powerful opposition.

One of the most consistent features of church history is the realization of the faithful that they are sustained by God. The opposition of men can be borne because of the support of God. This does not guarantee the safety of the church or the success of her efforts, but it does assure the church of sharing in the same power that raised Jesus from the grave—the self-emptying power of God's ministry to men. The power of Satan, the power of darkness, is the power of self-assertion and aggression. That power is opposed by the power of God, the power of light, which is the power of self-denial and service. The church is always tempted to turn away from the power of God and adopt the power of men. But when the church takes the sword, she perishes with the sword.

In her struggle against unfaithfulness she is allowed only one weapon—the cross. When the church has taken the cross, she has died to Satan, to darkness, to self-assertion and aggression, but she has lived to God, to light, to self-denial and service. Like Paul the church has "had the help that comes from God." The "help that comes from God" does not guarantee deliverance from opposition and persecution, but it does assure the church that there is no experience of life, not even death, which can separate God's faithful people from his presence and power.

■ Close the session by singing the hymn "Rise Up, O Men of God" (*The Methodist Hymnal,* 174).
■ Let the leadership team be prepared to give assignments for the next chapter of study and the members of the group be prepared to accept the assignments.

NOTES ON CHAPTER 10

Page 148: From "The Prison and the Angel" by Henry Van Dyke in *The Poems of Henry Van Dyke* (Charles Scribner's Sons, 1924), page 275.

The Spirit of Jesus has been released in the world and seeks embodiment in every aspect of the world's life.

11

□□□□□□□□□□□□□□□□ⁿⁿ□□□□□□□□□□□□□□□□□□□□□□□□

THE STATURE OF THE FULLNESS OF CHRIST

A sure sign that an individual is beginning to come of age as a person is his rebellion against external forms of discipline.

Most of us adults can remember our own youthful struggles to break away from the rules and regulations imposed upon us by those in positions of authority—parents, teachers, and such persons. We also are brought into the struggle from the other side as we see our own children and students seeking to become responsibly free of the control that we have exercised over their lives. As adults, we often deplore what seems to us to be a senseless and wasteful turning away from what we know is best. But our deploring of this sign of growth

■ *As you arrive at your place of meeting, check the assignment chart for specific preparation to be made before the session begins.*

■ Set goals for your study of this chapter as suggested on page 17.

in the young will not stop the process and will not lessen the tension that it causes.

One thing is absolutely certain: growing young people are going to keep on rebelling against adult authority, because it is one of the ways for them to become mature and responsible human beings. (*S/R*, 93.)

Does this mean that discipline has no place in a mature and responsible life? The answer is emphatically no! Vigorous and regular discipline must be applied anywhere excellence is required. When we watch a professional football player burst through the line of scrimmage, break into the clear, and race into the end zone for a touchdown, we see the results of years of physical and mental concentration.

This is not to suggest that any one of us by discipline alone can become whatever we decide. It means only that talent, whether great or small, requires discipline to be fully expressed.

Growing up certainly involves the young person in struggles against externally imposed discipline, but at the same time it thrusts upon the young person the necessity of finding some more adequate form of discipline. No person is really mature until he has substituted a voluntary system of rules and regulations for those that are imposed upon him. *Our task as adults is not to keep a tight rein on our youngsters but rather to show them the freedom and responsibility that result from living disciplined lives.* One of the reasons some of us seek to keep our children under external control is that deep down in our hearts we know that we have failed to develop a sound pattern of internal discipline in our own lives. Because we have never quite grown into mature adults, we do not trust our children to discipline their own lives.

■ Have five persons read as dialogue *S/R*, 94, with one serving as narrator. Then in the whole group give evidence for and against the statement in italics above.

The problem of discipline is not just a problem for the young. It is a problem for the immature of all ages. The full seriousness of the problem is really not understood until we set it in the context of our social relationships. The undisciplined home is a place of confusion and self-indulgence. But a home where discipline is imposed by the tyranny of absolute parental authority is marked by resentment, unrest, and often outright rebellion. The same is true of every unit of our society. Lack of discipline is ultimately destructive of every form of community life.

But the answer to the problem of an undisciplined society is not to impose more and more external restrictions and regulations. Every ordered society must have rules and restraints; but rules and restraints are not an end in themselves. They must always be used to help the persons involved grow from undisciplined self-assertion and indulgence into mature and responsible self-denial and service.

The church as a community like any other social system is faced with the problem of discipline. The problem is unusually acute in most modern Protestant churches, because the freedom and rights of the individual have been emphasized more than the claims and interests of the community. Most Protestant churches in the United States are loosely organized associations of individuals who think and act largely as they please. It is a known fact that service clubs and fraternities make more rigorous demands upon their members than the average Protestant church. The result is that our churches have become centers of undisciplined floundering and make little or no impact upon the shape of our society. (*S/R*, 95.)

■ Ask a previously appointed committee, who have found out the facts from the pastor or the commission on membership and evangelism, to report on your local church's program for adult membership training. Discuss the significance for your church of *S/R*, 95. How could your church strengthen your program? Why should a *training* program be necessary? A packet of materials for new church members is available from the General Board of Evangelism, 1908 Grand Avenue, Nashville, Tennessee 37202. Write that board for information.

But the problem is not new. It appeared very early in the history of the Christian church and has been a concern in each succeeding generation. For example, the author of the Letter to the Ephesians was aware of the undisciplined and self-indulgent patterns of behavior that were crippling the ministry of the church in the latter part of the first century. In Ephesians 4:1-16 he faced the problem head on. What he wrote in that passage was a call to disciplined participation in the community of faith. We consider it now because it speaks to our condition and suggests how we in our time may grow from childish self-assertion into mature and responsible membership in the life of the church.

THERE IS ONE BODY

The call to a disciplined life was a matter of pressing concern. The urgency arose from the fact that it rested not upon the insight of the author but upon the power and presence of God in human life. The "calling to which you have been called" (Ephesians 4:1) was a reference to God's gracious disclosure of himself in the life, death, and resurrection of Jesus. God had taken the initiative in establishing a community in which men could live faithfully and obediently.

The response that was demanded was not a vague commitment to religious ideas; rather, the response must be a *life* that corresponded to what God had done in Jesus Christ, "a life worthy of the calling to which you have been called." This meant one was to live according to the style of Jesus— "with all lowliness and meekness, with patience, forbearing one another in love."

164

These were not private virtues but the marks of life in community. In Jesus Christ God had not called men to a private and individual relationship. (S/R, 96.) Instead, he had called them to a community in which they were to receive and reveal that quality of life which characterized God's relationship to men.

Ephesians 4:2-3 helps us to see the necessity for a continued emphasis upon the place of discipline in the life of the church. The urgency with which we consider the subject of discipline does not arise from some external source but from the fact that in Jesus Christ we have been claimed by a new quality of life. "With all lowliness and meekness, with patience, forbearing" each one of us "in love," Jesus Christ has called us from our rebellion against God and our separation from our neighbors into a community of obedience to God and service to our neighbors. This community is the church. In it we are required to show the same quality of life which we have seen in the life of the Lord.

If this understanding were taken seriously in the life of the church, what a difference it would make! For one thing, it would mean the end of the loose and undisciplined attitude toward church membership that is so widespread today. An individual's relationship to Jesus Christ would no longer be viewed as a private matter but would be seen in the context of all his social relationships. It would also mean the submission of one's life to the disciplined demands of obeying God and loving neighbor. But who is responsible for seeing that this understanding is taken seriously? Each of us is responsible; because what God has done for one he has done for all.

The quarrels that plague many congregations and the jealousy that hinders much interdenominational co-operation suggest that we have been eager to promote our own interests and have failed to embody that Spirit of love which is the foundation of our true peace. In our own denomination it is extremely difficult to generate any enthusiasm for union with other denominations that would require us to revise our polity or renew our doctrines. The projects that are eagerly supported in the average local congregation often are expressions of competition for the most prominent place in the community. We have been eager to maintain the spirit of rivalry in the struggle to build finer buildings and attract larger congregations. The discipline that is lacking in the church today is devotion to Jesus Christ which expresses itself in deeds of self-denial and service. (S/R, 97.)

■ Ask several persons to read some of these other Scripture passages expressing what it means to live "a life worthy of the calling": (1) Galatians 5:22–6:6; (2) Romans 12:9-21; (3) Philippians 3:7-20; (4) Colossians 3:5-17; (5) 1 Thessalonians 5:12-22.
   Compare these with S/R, 97 and write your own definition of the Christian way.
■ Circular response (each person responds in order) : What do you know about the Methodist-EUB union? (See general church publications for information.)
■ What proposals for action and service have come from this group or others in the congregation during the last six months? Have a committee check to see how these recommendations are being carried out. Be sure to avoid judging another group's failure—the point is to get service and action going.
   What follow-up is needed? What new start can be made?

The situation in the church today is urgent, but it is not hopeless. Undisciplined churchmanship has wrought havoc in the life of the church, but reform and renewal are not impossible. The force that is supporting the unity of obedience in the church is more powerful than those forces that seek to divide her in disobedience. The call to disciplined participation in the life of the church is a powerful and creative force, because it rests squarely upon the unity of God himself. True community of faith and service is possible because God has released in human history those redemptive forces that enable men to believe in him and to love each other.

■ Show the filmslip "Getting Inside the Bible," frames 8-14 (Resource Packet, item 1, Script One). Read aloud in unison the script for these frames. (In co-operation with leadership teams from other groups in your church, have this portion of the script mimeographed.) Then in small groups discuss: Which of the frames most nearly express your idea of God's Word to us through the Bible today? Why do you choose these frames?

GRACE WAS GIVEN TO EACH OF US

One of the problems confronted by the author of Ephesians was the failure of many members of the church "to lead a life worthy of the calling to which" they had "been called." The possibility for participating responsibly in the community of faith had been given to each member of the church. Therefore, the task of maintaining "the unity of the Spirit in the bond of peace" was an obligation that none could escape. "But grace was given to each of us according to the measure of Christ's gift" (Ephesians 4:7). This verse emphasizes that the fullness of what God had done in Christ to establish one body, one Spirit, one hope, one Lord, one faith, and one baptism is operative in the life of each individual believer.

The writer's argument in this passage was based upon his faith in Jesus as the risen Lord. In his own experience in the church he had seen that the servant ministry of Jesus had not ended with his death on a cross. Through the power of the Resurrection Jesus had triumphed over the grave and continued as the creative and sustaining force in the life of his faithful followers. To express this fundamental reality and to bring it to bear upon the problem of discipline in the church, the author quoted from Psalms 68:18:

167

Therefore it is said,
> "When he ascended on high he led a
>   host of captives,
> and he gave gifts to men"
>   (Ephesians 4:8) .

By interpreting Jesus' ministry as a fulfillment of this Old Testament reference, the writer of Ephesians affirmed that the suffering, death, and resurrection of Jesus had been given by God as the most powerful force in human history. The victory that had been won by Jesus was not his only, but it was also the means whereby God had set free all who were bound by sin and death. In the ascension of Jesus—his exaltation—the church proclaimed that in her experience of the risen Lord she had been delivered from captivity and had been given the inspiration and the strength to lead a free and responsible life.

The ascension was the doctrine used by the church to proclaim that God had let loose the Spirit of Jesus in the world "that he might fill all things" (Ephesians 4:10*b*) . The author of this passage had caught a glimpse of God's power and purpose. This vision of invincible might and of unlimited good will prompted him to call for a similar dedication on the part of all those who were joined to him in the one body of faith, the church.

There is nothing to be gained by laboring the point that the church today is crippled by the undisciplined behavior of her members. Those of us who have worked faithfully in the church are painfully aware of our own shortcomings. It is not good news to be hemmed in by the evidence that we have not led "a life worthy of the calling to which" we "have been called." Here the author of Ephesians ministers to our need. He proclaims the gospel of our release which is more powerful than the bad news of our failure. The word of encouragement which God speaks through this passage is that God himself is at work in the weakness, rebellion, and sin of the church. He "is above all and through all and in all" and that means he is not absent from our quarrels and divisions but powerfully present in *all* our needs.

WE ARE TO GROW UP IN EVERY WAY

As the author of Ephesians surveyed the life of the first-century church, he recognized that the unity God intended for his people was not to be realized by everyone performing the same service. There are many kinds of service. He began the development of this thought by applying it to the ministry of those who had been set apart to perform specific functions in the church. "And his gifts were that some should be apostles, some prophets, some evangelists, some pastors and teachers" (Ephesians 4:11). These were specialized ministries in the early church.

Today we take it for granted that certain people are set apart in the church to perform special tasks. Those who serve in performing these tasks are in "specialized ministries" in our day. We must be careful not to think too highly or too lowly of the place that such persons occupy in the life of the church. We think too highly of them when we assume that they have some preferable relationship to the body of Christ. We think too lowly of them when we forget that they have been equipped by Christ himself to perform those functions that the normal growth of the body requires.

The ministers in our churches today are members of the one body in exactly the same way as all other members. They are different from other members only in the sense that they have received gifts that enable them to perform such special tasks as preaching and teaching and leading in worship.

It would be a mistake to think of these special tasks as fixed and settled once and for all by the patterns that were effective in the first century. The body grows. The needs of the body are therefore changing constantly. The specialized

169

ministries of the set-apart members must also change to meet those needs. One of the most pressing and critical problems in the life of today's church is the tendency to put the clergy in the strait jacket of outmoded forms of ministry and to refuse to permit them to serve the needs of a changing situation. (S/R, 98.)

Our challenge is quite different from that which the author of Ephesians faced. The set-apart or ordained ministry is now an established part of church life. The challenge we face is how to free those who minister as clergy from the traditional expectations and images that keep them from meeting the real needs of the church. For example, the average congregation clings to the notion that preaching is the most important task performed by the clergy. But there is good evidence to support the idea that in our present situation the most important function of the ordained ministry is teaching. It is not necessary to debate the issue here. The point is simply that we must keep our minds open to the fact that Christ's gifts have begun specialized ministries in the church. These ministries are to meet the needs of a growing body. When a particular ministry is no longer needed, it should be discarded to make a place for a new ministry that *is* needed. We should not continue any form of ministry merely because we are comfortable with it. The discipline that is demanded of all the members of the body is faithful openness to the future in which the only certainty is the change of growth.

■ Have a panel of persons ready to present various sides of this issue: "Pastors should stick to preaching on personal salvation, to pastoral work, and to administration instead of preaching on social issues, joining controversial groups, and involving themselves in community problems." Give evidence—each panelist might interview several ministers. (See also *S/R*, 98 and Jeremiah 26:1-19.)

The tasks that the clergy are called to perform in the church may very well change from time to time, but the overriding purpose of whatever the clergy do remains constant: to serve the body of Christ. The questions that arise about the work of the ordained ministry in today's church are: Does the ministry really equip the other members for their ministry and does it really build up the body of Christ? The gifts that Christ has given to those engaged in specialized ministries are not to be used in coddling and pampering the church. They are to be used to prepare the church to fulfill her ministry in the world. (*S/R*, 99.) The clergy are commissioned to serve the body of Christ in order that the whole body will become an effective instrument to accomplish Christ's purpose in the world.

One of the inescapable responsibilities of the clergy is that of disciplining the life of the body. The authority that the clergy exercise in the church is *not* the authority of external rules and regulations. It is the internal authority, one that grows out of common commitment to a common cause. Since the clergy have been equipped by Christ himself for their service in the church, they cannot shirk their disciplinary responsibilities without rebelling against the Lord. Likewise, the discipline that the clergy administer in the church is the gift of Christ to the whole body. If the members reject this discipline of Christ, they are actually guilty of rebelling against the will of Christ for his body.

■ Read *S/R*, 99 silently. In groups of four, compare the authority of the minister in the reading with the view presented above. Then converse on the question: What is your earliest childhood recollection of the minister as authority? How can the minister's authority best be exercised? How channeled? How strengthened? How supported *NOW*?

Or several persons might interview various ministers on their understanding of their authority, and report findings. If ministerial authority has declined, why has it?

What changes in our understanding of the "ministry of the clergy" might make a more effective church? How can we avoid the idea that the local church "hires" the minister?

171

The need for discipline in the church is not a popular subject. We would prefer to ignore it or dismiss it as an impractical ideal. Of course, there are always dangers in any attempt to exercise discipline in the church. It can easily become the occasion for automatic and tyrannical control or it can just as easily be used to promote self-righteous hypocrisy. These dangers, however, are not nearly so real and present as the irresponsibility and ineffectiveness that cripple the church when she fails to use the ministries that Christ has established to discipline her own life. The body of Christ requires such discipline, because the members are not perfect. Because we do not fully realize Christ's purpose for our lives, we do not make our proper contribution to the normal functioning and growth of the body.

So that no man might conclude that he had achieved "mature manhood," the writer of Ephesians pointed out that all men have unlimited possibilities for growth. Life in the body of Christ had as its goal the development of each member until all attained "to the measure of the stature of the fullness of Christ." There can be little doubt that what the author had in mind here was Christ's absolute dependence upon God expressed in his unlimited love for men. Each member of the body of Christ had been created for this purpose, and the life of the entire body was incomplete until this purpose was realized in every part.

The good news proclaimed in this passage is that in Jesus Christ God had acted to restore men to their true humanity and that through the ministries which he had established in the church he continued to lead men from immature unfaithfulness to mature faithfulness, "to the measure of the stature of the fullness of Christ."

WHAT ARE OUR GOALS?

One of the most significant results of studying a passage such as Ephesians 4:1-16 is that it compels us to examine

172

the goals which we have set for ourselves in the church. God wills unity for us. When we settle for divisions and brokenness, we frustrate his purpose and deny his will. God calls us in the church "to the unity of the faith and of the knowledge of the Son of God." Moreover, he is actively present in the specialized ministries of the church, giving of himself so that we might be faithful and so that our lives might be ruled by our relationship to his Son.

■ Let a committee pose to the official board these questions and bring a report to the group:

1. Does our church have any stated goals?

2. How would you state the goals of our local church, on the basis of Ephesians 4:1-16 and the Order for Confirmation and Reception into the Church (*The Methodist Hymnal*)?

After their report, discuss these questions:

1. What do you understand by "unity" in the local church, as interpreted in the text above?

2. What examples of brokenness and division do you see in your church? How does this division hinder movement toward your stated goals?

3. What are the *actual* goals of your church as seen in its total influence? How are they different from the *stated* goals?

4. How do your goals contribute to, or hinder, the movement of the whole church toward unity?

In recent years we have seen a concerted effort to popularize theology and to make the insights of scholars available to all students of the Bible. This commendable program has brought to light a regrettable childishness and immaturity in the church. For example, in the "God is dead" controversy many members of our churches were "tossed to and fro and carried about" (Ephesians 4:14) by the opinions that were expressed in the course of the discussion. It is not my purpose here to debate the validity of the various theological positions that have been identified with the "God is dead" issue. My purpose here is merely to observe that the eagerness with which some churchmen embraced this novelty and the frantic defensiveness with which some rejected it were both in-

173

dicative of widespread childishness and immaturity in the church. If we had been prepared by disciplined efforts to "attain to the unity of the faith and of the knowledge of the Son of God, to mature manhood," we would have been able to approach the issues raised as opportunities for continued growth in the body of Christ.

The way for us to overcome our childishness is certainly not the way of the closed mind that shuts out every new thought. The road to "mature manhood" is a pilgrimage characterized by that faith in God and love for neighbor which allow men to change their thoughts and words and deeds without losing their way.

In Ephesians 4:15-16 the writer has shifted the focus of his concern from the discipline supplied by specialized ministries to the discipline each member was expected to exercise in relationship to all other members of the body. An evidence of growth and maturity in the body was the responsibility that each member accepted for correcting and encouraging all the other members. An indispensable element in the care of the members for each other was the willingness to risk "speaking the truth in love." This kind of fundamental honesty and acceptance of each other was a means of grace which enabled each member to become aware of his need for continued growth and which also enabled each member to give and receive the help "to grow up in every way into him who is the head, into Christ."

The points of contact between the concluding verses of this passage and the present-day church are too numerous to mention. It almost seems that the author had our particular situation in mind when he wrote these words. A few suggestions will serve to point up the relevance of his message for our contemporary church life. His plea for "speaking the truth in love" illumines the deceit and shallowness of much of our life together in the church. We are afraid to speak genuine words of encouragement or of rebuke.

174

To overcome this crippling weakness many congregations have organized small groups that are units of mutual support. These groups at their best are characterized by trust and acceptance which enable the members to be absolutely honest with each other. The result of such groups is that the participants realize where and how they need to grow and are also able to find the help from one another to assist their growth. These small groups are a sign that the church is beginning to recover the understanding that her growth is not a matter of private and individual development but a matter of the whole body of the church maturing through the proper functioning of all its parts.

There is good news here for us. The gospel is not that the members of the body have "to grow up in every way into him who is the head, into Christ." The gospel is that the head, Christ, has accepted us as members of his body and that his powerful ministry includes the *whole* body, *every* joint, *each* part. The head cares for the parts in their division, in their immaturity, even in their rebellion and disobedience. Freed of the burden of self-justification, each part is joined and knit together with every other part. The whole body enjoys the health that comes from the proper functioning of all its parts.

■ Use "The Nineteenth Hole" (Resource Packet, item 8) to evaluate your progress toward the ideal expressed in the preceding paragraph.
■ Close with a silent prayer for your minister (s) .
■ Let the leadership team be prepared to give assignments for the next chapter of study and the members of the group be prepared to accept the assignments.

175

Each of us has experienced some upheaval in his life so utterly devastating that life seems empty and meaningless.

12

□□

MORE THAN CONQUERORS

In the chapters of this book we have attempted to listen for the good news that is proclaimed in the biblical passages we have studied together. Our primary purpose has not been to transmit information about the Bible but to read and hear its *witness* to the good news—the judging and redeeming presence of God in our lives.

We have come to see that from the biblical point of view the good news is not something men have said or written about God but what God has done for men to inspire them to trust him and to love each other. The biblical words are important because they point to those decisive events in which faithful men have discovered God's revelation of himself and his way. The climax of God's manifestation of himself is the life, death, and resurrection of Jesus. In the life and work of Jesus we are given the full and complete dis-

---

■ *As you arrive at your place of meeting, check the assignment chart for specific preparation to be made before the session begins.*

■ Set goals for your study of this chapter as suggested on page 17.

closure of God's gracious power and presence in our lives. His obedient service, his humiliation, and his victory over the grave are the means through which the word *Immanuel*— *God with us*—has become the gospel of our release from the bondage of sin and death.

But our release from the slavery of sin and death is not complete. The Bible does not speak to us as men who have won the final victory. It addresses us as men who are thrown into the heat of battle against a formidable and unrelenting foe. This is one of the points where the biblical message strikes a responsive chord in our own experience. We know that life itself is a struggle. There may be moments of relative quiet in the battle but as long as life continues the warfare knows no end. The danger is real and present; the foe is particular and personal. As individuals we are constantly threatened by the frailty of our health, anxiety about our work, inadequacy in our personal relationships, frustration in the face of complex social issues. Moreover, as members of society we are torn by the conflict of nation against nation, class against class, race against race, creed against creed. What is the relationship of the good news to these experiences that seem always about to overwhelm us? (*S/R,* 100.)

■ What is the relationship of the good news to the threats and conflicts experienced by persons as individuals and as members of society? Study the two teaching pictures displayed by the leadership team "Christ and Missile" and "Soldier With Bible" (Resource Packet, items 6 and 7). The Leaders' Guide in the packet provides specific directions for studying these pictures. Read silently *S/R,* 100. How can we make the good news relevant to our problems without falling into the habit of trying to match every problem with a specific Bible verse?

For some of us the grim realities of life appear so shatteringly powerful that they make it difficult for us to believe that God is with us. This is a shocking statement but until we are willing to face it there is little chance that the good news will penetrate to the deepest levels of our need and despair. If the gospel is *really* true, if God is *really* with us, then we no longer need to pretend that our faith is perfect. We can confidently confess that we have doubts and fears which seem to deny God's presence and power; for we know that unless God's good news is capable of meeting the test of our unfaithfulness, there is no gospel for us. This effort to put up a brave front is rejection of the good news because it shuts God out of the experiences where our need for help is most desperate and acute.

Each one of us has experienced or will experience some upheaval in his personal or social life so utterly devastating that life seems empty and meaningless. It is impossible to avoid such experiences. Literally, there is no place to hide, nowhere to run, no way out. (*S/R*, 101.) The good news of God does not take us out of those experiences that emphasize and underscore our need, but it helps us to see that precisely in such experiences God himself is powerfully present as our judge and redeemer.

One of the most eloquent witnesses to God's invincible presence in human history appears in Romans 8:28-39, the basis for our study of this chapter. These words of the apostle Paul show how he helped his readers to see that the darkest experiences of life had been claimed as the arena of God's saving action. We study them now in the hope that they will help us also to realize that there is no shadowy realm of our existence where the word *Immanuel* has not been made a reality through the life, death, and resurrection of Jesus.

IN EVERYTHING GOD WORKS FOR GOOD

In this passage Paul faced the challenge that those who had believed in Jesus Christ had not been delivered from the struggles of human existence. (*S/R*, 102.) If anything, the confession "Jesus Christ is Lord" had intensified rather

179

than lessened the struggle. Did this mean that the good news Paul had preached and the Romans had believed was false? Certainly not! With eyes wide open to the realities of the human condition, Paul declared, "We know that in everything God works for good with those who love him, who are called according to his purpose" (Romans 8:28). Paul affirmed this so emphatically that there must have been serious questions by some people. Apparently, some doubted that God's power and presence operated in the tribulation, distress, persecution, famine, nakedness, peril, and sword they had experienced. Seemingly, they had decided that these devastating experiences were signs that they had been cut off from God, that he was not really with them.

Paul did not meet this challenge by advancing arguments to prove that God was with his people in time of trouble. Instead, he appealed to the authority of his knowledge or experience of what God was doing in the world. In his life with the risen Lord, he had come to know that God was powerfully present not just in a few isolated moments of inspiration but in the whole sweep of man's joy and sorrow. (S/R, 103.) The revelation Paul had received through the life, death, and resurrection of Jesus had opened his eyes to the fact "that in everything God works for good."

This acceptance did not mean that he accepted everything as good. It meant that not even the evil that men did to each other could shut out the good God intended. Tribulation, distress, persecution, famine, nakedness, peril, and sword were evil and contrary to God's will, but these evils were not signs that God had deserted his people. Instead, they were signs that God had entered the struggle on their behalf and was working for their good in those experiences that seemed to threaten their very existence. The foundation of this faith was the ministry of Jesus. Just as he had entered fully into all the experiences of men while on earth, so now as the risen Lord he continued to share fully in everything that men experienced. (*S/R*, 104.)

■ In groups of six to eight persons study Romans 8:28-39. Consult biblical commentaries such as *The Interpreter's Bible*, volume 9. (Ask your minister to recommend resources.) Each group will conduct its study in the light of one of the following suggestions:

a. Cite several specific biblical examples of God's saving action in the midst of dark experiences. Then share similar personal experiences.

b. Read Romans 8:28-39; then read *S/R*, 102. What comfort would you receive from Romans 8:28 if you were in a similar situation? Cite some modern examples of costly discipleship. Recall the time when your witness cost you most.

c. Focus your study on verses 35 and 36. How can these evils be considered signs of God's presence rather than his absence? How are they the results of the evilness of man? What hope do you gain from *S/R*, 104?

d. Rewrite verses 35 and 38-39 as a twentieth-century writer might write them.

As we face the challenge that the struggle for existence brings to us, the most important resource of our faith is not what we know about ourselves but what we know about God. In the life, death, and resurrection of Jesus we have seen "that in everything God works for good." This statement must be taken quite literally. Above all, it must be affirmed that there is no darkness powerful enough to shut out the light of God's presence. Precisely in the midst of suffering, injustice, hatred, and inhumanity God works for good by giving himself for the needs of men. The good news that Paul proclaims in this verse of Scripture is that evil is not all-powerful. God claimed it for the realm of his saving work and uses it as the means for accomplishing his will.

This does not mean that evil is to be accepted. It means that evil must be attacked wherever it is found and, more importantly, that it is being attacked and overthrown by the all-conquering love of God in Jesus Christ. Men are not left alone by God to struggle against forces that are too much for them. Men are called by God to join *with him* in his work for good. As we look out upon our own world of distress and despair, we see men and women committed to the task of relieving human suffering and securing a better life for all the members of the family of man. In their humble service we see more than the works of men. (*S/R*, 105.) We see also "that in everything God works for good with those who love him, who are called according to his purpose."

■ In preparing for this session each person should clip from a magazine or newspaper a picture that illustrates the idea that wherever evil is being attacked, God works for good. Let persons share their pictures with the entire group or if the group is very large, in small groups, and tell why they chose that particular picture. Display the pictures on a bulletin board or blank wall under the caption, posted in advance by the leadership team, "Wherever evil is being attacked, God works for good." Discuss: How do these pictures differ from the "normal" activity of the church?

When we read Paul today, we find that his subordination of everything to the sovereign power of God is not so easily acceptable to our contemporary way of viewing human life. This Pauline point of view comes to full voice in the next verse of this passage: "For those whom he foreknew he also predestined to be conformed to the image of his Son, in order that he might be the first-born among many brethren" (Romans 8:29). (*S/R*, 106.)

What was Paul saying in this language that is so strange to our modern ears? To begin with, he was giving his faithful explanation of the fact that in Jesus Christ God had succeeded in creating a people who shared with him in his work for good. The existence of such a people in human history was the result of God's sovereign power. They had not discovered God. He had known them and his knowledge or dealing with them was the foundation of their existence.

We must seek now to relate this strange language about foreknowledge and predestination to our own experience.

182

First, let us agree that our purpose is not to defend or attack a doctrine but to shed light on the significance of an experience. The point of contact between this verse and our present situation is our life together in the church. However weakly and imperfectly, our participation in the life of the church is a sign that God has gathered us around him to share in his work for good. How do we account for the miracle of our participation in this new community?

In the strange language of Paul, God has foreknown us; that is, he has given himself to us in love so that we may have faith in him and love each other. The quality of life accepted as standard behavior in the new community of faith is nothing less than conformity to the image of God's Son. We accept this standard for our relationships with each other, not because we have made a decision on our own. Rather, it is possible because God is at work in our lives in the self-giving power of his Son.

In the language of Paul, God has predestined us for suffering service by loving us and giving his Son for us. Jesus of Nazareth is not an isolated event in ancient history. On the contrary, he is the revelation of God's sovereign power which raises us from death to life and establishes us in a community where we are his brethren.

Notice in Romans 8:30 how Paul pressed home his faith that in God's sovereign power his people were provided with the resources they needed to join him in his work for good. "And those whom he predestined he also called; and those whom he called he also justified; and those whom he justified he also glorified."

One of the problems that Paul recognized in this particular verse was the agony of those who were treated as criminals because of their obedience to God. Because they had accepted God's way for their lives, they had been rejected by the powerful and respected persons of society. By being with God where he was revealing himself and by joining him in what he was doing in the world, they had called down upon their heads the condemnation of the world.

How could they justify themselves before men? The answer of this verse was very clear. They no longer had to trouble themselves to justify themselves before men, because they had been justified by God. God was with them. He had chosen them to be with him in his work for good in the world. The rejection by men was no longer a cause of anxiety, because they had been accepted by God. Separation from the society of men was no longer exile, because they had been received into the promised land of knowing and doing the will of God.

■ What are the risks in accepting God's way? Working in pairs or small groups, specify (write out) a series of possible consequences that might result if on the basis of his/her acceptance of God's acceptance of him/her:

a. A coach decides to teach his boys to be better boys rather than to be winners at any price.

b. An editor of a newspaper decides to make his paper a vehicle to work for justice for all people rather than reflect the vested interests of the power structures of the community.

c. A housewife decides to make only positive remarks about persons who become the subject of gossip at the neighborhood coffee.

Each team or group will work with only one of the examples. Report your conclusions to the group. How might Romans 8:28-39 offer assurance in these cases?

You might decide to dramatize the consequences of these three situations through role plays.

The rewards of position and status and recognition in the kingdoms of the world had been taken from them. How could they adjust to a life stripped of its splendor? The answer given by Paul was a redefinition of the glory (the splendor) of the Christian life based upon his understanding of the lordship of Jesus. Jesus was Lord not in the sense of worldly power and grandeur but in the sense of his complete commitment to the will of his Father. God's will was that men be served. The glory of Jesus was revealed in his life of service, in his obedience unto death, even death on a cross. The splendor that the followers of Jesus possessed was participation with him in working for good by giving their lives in loving service. (*S/R*, 107.) God had glorified them by releasing in them the power that enabled them to conform to the image of his Son. In short, they had been released from striving for the glory of this world through the gift of God's glory.

■ Let members of the group cite illustrations to show that the "average Christian" is or is not free from the desire for status and recognition in society. When might a reasonable amount of desire for status and recognition be good?

How free are you from the desire for status and recognition? Complete the following statements. This will not be shared with the group, so be perfectly honest with yourself.

a. Of all the *awards* I might receive I would rather receive

_____.

b. Of all the types of *recognition* I might receive I would rather be recognized _____.

c. Of all the *services* I might perform I would rather do _____

_____.

d. Of all the *groups* from which I might receive acclaim I would rather have the acclaim of _____

_____.

How does the kind of glory and honor reflected in your answers compare with the description of glory and honor above? How is this kind of glory to be experienced by members of your group?

WHO IS AGAINST US?

"If God is for us, who is against us?" (Romans 8:31*b*) suggested that from the standpoint of the gospel there was no possibility of God's people experiencing defeat. Romans 8:28-39 must be read against the background of charges that the Christians were enemies of God and foes of humanity. Paul himself had been accused of blasphemy and insurrection. Therefore, it was only natural that out of personal involvement he should ask, "Who shall bring any charge against God's elect?" (Romans 8:33*a*). The point of the question was simply that God's approval made the accusations of men of no account. This thought reminded Paul of what he had already said in verse 30. "It is God who justifies; who is to condemn?" (Romans 8:33*b*-34*a*).

Again he was driven back in his thought to rest his entire case upon what God had done in Jesus Christ. The ability of the church to stand the test of human existence was based upon the reality of her Lord's ministry for her. The form was a question but the content was a fervent affirmation: "Is it Christ Jesus, who died, yes, who was raised from the dead, who is at the right hand of God, who indeed intercedes for us?" (Romans 8:34*b, c*). The suffering service of Jesus did not end in death. It was the most powerful force in the universe. It had broken the bonds of death, had called the church into existence, and continued to serve the church in her time of testing.

Thus Paul came once again to the heart of the matter: "Who shall separate us from the love of Christ?" (Romans 8:35*a*). The question had been posed by the hard realities of the situation. The presence of Christ with his people had called forth the massive opposition of all the forces of evil. Paul did not view these evils as impersonal; they were personal threats to human existence. He listed them one by one as he surveyed the experiences that he had shared with his readers: "Shall tribulation, or distress, or persecution, or famine, or nakedness, or peril, or sword?" (Romans 8:35*b*).

God had condescended to accept the full limitations of human existence that included exposure to the power of evil. Therefore, men of faith participated in the shattering experiences of life (being killed all the day long and regarded as sheep to be slaughtered) not in spite of the power of God but because in Christ the power of God was revealed in the way he became completely human and knew human need. "For thy sake," that is, for the sake of the God, "who did not spare his own Son but gave him up for us all," men of faith gave themselves up to tribulation, distress, persecution, famine, nakedness, peril, and sword. Paul could write this and his readers could receive it because they knew "that in everything God works for good with those who love him." The answer to the question posed by the struggles of human existence was given by God himself.

These verses suggest the response that we should make to the good news of God's presence and power in our lives. The realization that "God is for us" helps us to see the struggles of life in proper perspective. We can face the conflict without fear because we know that we are not alone. God is *with* us and *for* us.

God's people today are beset by powerful and pervasive forces of evil. This fact will surely plunge us into despair unless we hold fast to the assurance that our enemies are more than matched by the fact that our ally in the warfare is God himself. Because he is for us, those who are against us count for nothing. Our ability to stand the testing of our time is not dependent upon our loyalty and commitment but upon the loyalty and commitment of God. We know that he has chosen us, because he "did not spare his own Son but gave him up for us all." We also know that whatever we need to live as faithful men will be given to us through the ministry of his Son.

In our own country, faithfulness to God often results in false charges and unfounded accusations being made. For example, men of faith who attempt to relate the good news to our economic problems are often called communists. How can the Christian stand firm in the presence of such attacks and make his witness without fear? He can only do this by understanding that he has been called (elected) by God to make his witness at this time and in relation to these particular human needs. (S/R, 108.)

His obedience to God and his dependence upon God's power enable him to see that the accusations of men have no bearing on what he is and does. The fact that God has chosen him and given him this task is the only justification he requires. Since he has the approval of God, the disapproval of men is of no consequence. Moreover, the all-conquering ministry of Jesus' life, death, and resurrection continues to release the power of God in the life of his faithful followers. The suffering service of Jesus guarantees that those who serve in his name are supported and sustained by God himself.

■ The attempt of men of faith to relate the good news to contemporary issues often arouses suspicions and brings verbal attacks. Jesus faced the same problem. Read Matthew 12:9-14.

Now, meet Charley Christian. Let one person read aloud S/R, 108 while another pantomimes (goes through the actions but does not speak) the character in the reading.

Jesus has something to say to the "Charleys" of his day. Listen while one member reads Matthew 23:1-15, 23-28. Then read silently S/R, 107.

In the light of what you have just read, seen, and heard, how would you answer the person who says, "The church should stick to teaching and preaching the 'simple gospel' and not get mixed up in economic, social, and political problems"? How can the Christian react to verbal attacks and accusations? Based on your understanding of Romans 8:28-39, what assurance and support could and would you offer a person under attack?

I AM SURE

Paul wrote Romans 8:28-39 because he was uncertain about the ability of his readers to meet the test of life's struggle. I think also he was doubtful about the adequacy of his own strength. It is all the more remarkable, therefore, that he did not emphasize the doubts and fears that threatened to overwhelm him and his readers. He began this passage by writing "we know" and he concluded it by affirming "for I am sure." The reason Paul was able to break out of the prison of human frailty and weakness was that his life was founded upon the assurance and power of what God had done for him in Christ Jesus his Lord.

Romans 8:38-39 is the summary of Paul's own experience of how God's presence triumphed over everything that appeared to shut him out of human life. (S/R, 109.) The dangers in the present moment and the threats of what was about to happen were powerless to shake his confidence in God, because God was with him in self-giving love which satisfied all his needs. The sovereign power of God was the fundamental fact of his existence. Before that fact all other powers, those from above, or below, or anywhere in the whole creation, were rendered insignificant.

How had Paul attained this certainty? It had been given to him through his experience of Jesus as the risen Lord. The fact that the risen Lord had disclosed himself to Paul was evidence not only that God had come into human experience in the past but also that he continued to give himself in all the distress and need of human life. Christ Jesus was Lord because he had conquered death, life, angels, principalities, things present, things to come, powers, height, depth, and everything in all creation.

The reason we need to read this passage and listen for its message is that like Paul we too have no assurance about ourselves. As we examine our lives, we find very little to suggest that our strength is sufficient for the trials we must face in this world. How then can we stand? The answer is given not by dwelling at length upon our doubts and fears but by fixing our attention upon him whose revelation of himself conquers our uncertainties about ourselves. We may not be able to hold fast to God, but we are sure that he holds fast to us. Moreover, we can admit that we are not perfectly faithful because we know that he is always faithful.

This is not whistling in the dark. But it is affirming by faith that his abiding presence makes the darkness bright as day. This faith has been created in us by what God did and does in Christ Jesus our Lord. Jesus has entered and enters the mysterious realm of death and, therefore, we do not go alone into the unknown but journey with him who is our inseparable companion. Jesus has shared and shares all the experiences of our common life. So we do not run from life but embrace it in the confidence that whatever happens Jesus will be disclosed more fully to us.

Of course, there are forces that we do not understand. We cannot explain them away and perhaps we may never be rid of them. However, we do not lose hope because we know that they also have been defeated by our Lord and will be brought at last to recognize his majesty and glory. The anxiety of life in the present and the fear of life in the future are now bearable because in Christ we have received and are receiving all that we need to live faithfully and meaningfully. The powerful presence of the risen Lord in our lives and in our world means that there is no power anywhere in the whole creation which can defeat the saving work God has begun and continues in us. Since we share with Paul the benefits of the good news, we can say with Paul, "I am sure that nothing in all creation will be able to separate us from the love of God in Christ Jesus our Lord."

Immanuel, "God with us," is not a fond hope; it is the fundamental reality of human experience. The Bible as witness to the good news of God's loving presence with us does not transport us to some otherworldly realm. Instead, it transforms us here in this world by helping us to become faithful witnesses to what God is doing in us, through us, and for us. The climax of our study of the Bible is reached when "the love of God in Christ Jesus our Lord" has become so real that "we know that in everything God works for good with those who love him, who are called according to his purpose."

■ This entire study has been built around the idea that the Bible witnesses to the good news. To get a panoramic view of the Bible as good news, review the twelve key passages. Divide the group into twelve small groups, or pairs. Each group will read the assigned scriptural passage and decide why it is good news for them. Limit this part of the procedure to five minutes. Then share ideas with the entire group.

■ Close the session by reading silently the last three paragraphs of this book and then reading in unison Romans 8:35-39.

■ The author and the editors hope you have used the materials and suggestions of this unit freely. We hope you have taken more than a quarter for your study. If you do have time for another session before beginning the third unit of Foundation Studies, we suggest you go back and try some of the procedures you omitted. Or read together some of the Selected Readings you missed, or repeat some procedures that might have more meaning for you now.